# THE DAY MY SHORTS
# FIT MY DAD

# THE DAY MY SHORTS FIT MY DAD

## Adventures of a Former Fat Chick

SUZANNE BERKEY

Palmetto Publishing Group, LLC
Charleston, SC

Quantity sales are available on quantity purchases. For details email
the publisher at: info@thewarriorwithinme.com

ISBN-13: 978-1-944313-05-0
ISBN-10: 1944313052

First Edition

DISCLOSURE:

This book is designed to provide information and motivation to our readers. It is sold with the understanding that the publisher and author are not engaged to render any type of psychological, legal, or any other kind of professional advice. The content is the sole expression and opinion of its author, and not necessarily that of the publisher. No warranties or guarantees are expressed or implied by the publisher or author. Neither the publisher nor the individual author(s) shall be liable for any physical, psychological, emotional, financial, or commercial damages, including, but not limited to, special, incidental, consequential or other damages. Our views and rights are the same: You are responsible for your own choices, actions, and results.

*To My Husband, Jeff—*

*I am so grateful to have you on
this journey of life with me.
I am thankful that through our
laughter, tears, and fun that we get
to make many memories together.*

# Table of Contents

# Introduction: The Adventure Compass

LET'S FACE IT: Losing weight is hard. It seems like everyone is complaining about being overweight. But what if you need to lose some *serious* weight? Who are you going to listen to? Surely not those toothpick-thin girls who live on water and crackers.

Great news! This isn't some skinny-girl diet book. It's a real-life, hard-lesson-learning book written by someone who has traveled this road. It's a tell-all, humorous, non-calorie-counting book. Through reading the stories, you'll see that losing large amounts of weight *is* possible and *can* be done.

How do I know? Because I lived it. *The Day My Shorts Fit My Dad* is the story of the trials and tribulations I experienced while losing one hundred pounds, all while navigating ass-busting, life-changing challenges and victories. I have been there. Craving a giant two-story cupcake. Yep, that was me. Are you sneaking giant pieces of chocolate while walking around the block? Totally understand. I've been there. Losing the weight slowly but surely, one pound at a time, I experienced the feelings of frustration, happiness and being challenged all during one journey—sometimes in the same day or week.

Travel with me as I tell you about how being on this rollercoaster ride changed my life and the lives of those around me.

Women and men of all ages struggle with weight loss. We become discouraged, desperate to find *one* person who has been where we are. One person who knows about the temptation to eat an entire Costco-sized bag of chocolate chips. Someone who understands not wanting to get up and exercise for five seconds, let alone thirty minutes. We search for someone just like us who understands and can share examples of struggles and successes that make us *believe* weight loss is possible. I have written this book for that exact purpose!

I promise that if you travel this journey with me, you'll see that I'm not some skinny chick telling you to live off grapefruit and diuretics. This is an honest-to-goodness, hardworking, been-there-done-that journey of *real* weight loss. By the end of the book, you likely will have laughed, cried, and developed a sense of hope that you can lose the weight, too.

Don't be the person who waits until the last ounce of hope is gone. Be the person who wants to make a difference in his or her own life. Be the person who wants to be around for his or her children and grandchildren. Be the person who's ready to say, "It's *my* life, and *I am worth the change.*" Don't wait until the day you have no other options but to make a change. Do it because *you* say so. Do it *now*!

The trials, tribulations, and victories you're about to read are proven. I've experienced them, and so can you. Each chapter will provide tips and confessions on how I lost the hundred pounds. Take a chance on yourself now. Make *you* great!

# Adventure #1:
## The Dreaded Doctor Visits

---

I T WAS TIME for school-clothes shopping. My sister and I wandered around Sears, looking for clothes to wear. I wanted cute clothes. Cute jeans, a feminine t-shirt, beloved tennis shoes, or my favorite cowboy boots would have been nice. The problem was that in my size, there weren't a lot of cute clothes. I was a little chunky monkey, by 1970s standards, who was always covered in dirt, grease, or mud, and I was known for having my hand in the cookie jar too many times to count. We didn't have fast food in our little country town. We ate at home all the time, and it was something super special to get to have ice cream. We weren't even allowed to drink pop or Kool-Aid unless it were a special occasion.

My family isn't one of those families where being fat is hereditary. My sister is short and thin. My mom is average height and thin. And then there's me. I was just a normal kid who happened to have her dad's stature. My dad and I are about five-foot-seven (on a good day) and stocky. He has thick, strong, tree-trunk legs and super built calves. Sounds great, right? Not! Great stature for a male, but not so great when you are female. What it meant for me was that while growing up, I was aware of my build, but never felt fat or obese or anything of that nature. I just knew I was different. If I'd been a boy—which I got mistaken for often—I bet the football coach would have thought I'd be a great addition to the team.

Size didn't really become a problem for me until the summer before my freshman year of high school. We didn't own a scale in our house, so I had no way of knowing my actual weight. When it was time for my physical to play high-school sports, I learned that I might have a weight issue. Often the comments people make, even though they're meant to be harmless, will stick with you for a very long time.

In my small town, there was only one doctor. After my physical, the doctor stood next to me. I can specifically remember, he looked at me and said, "You have gained twenty pounds this year." To a beginning high-school freshman, I didn't know the significance of that statement. I wasn't sure if it was a good thing or bad thing, but based on the way he was looking at me with those shrewd little eyes and a frown on his face, I guessed it wasn't good. He went on to say that people of my height on average didn't weigh that much. *Weigh that much*? It wasn't as though I'd gained two hundred pounds. What's a measly twenty pounds in a year? Because being overweight wasn't really as prevalent as it is today, learning I had gained twenty pounds didn't really mean all that much. I didn't have any idea what I was supposed to weigh or what the guidelines were. He didn't really take the time to explain it to me either, but what I *can* tell you is that I felt devastated. In my mind, I can remember thinking, *He just called me fat*, and I didn't know how to respond. I was hurt. This small-statured doctor grabbed my thigh and said, "You can't gain that kind of weight. You may want to exercise." Exercise? Umm, hello! I was there to get a physical to play basketball. How much more exercise did I need? Was he suggesting that I needed to take up another sport? Was he telling me I was going to have to give up my infrequent Kool-Aid? I had no idea.

I came home from the doctor's office, and I didn't know what to say. I was ashamed that I had to explain to my mom that the doctor had called me fat. I was just trying to play high school basketball. Wasn't that the whole point—to be active? I was so confused and lost. All I could do was hope that with all the upcoming basketball practices, I would lose some weight. But in all honesty, the biggest thing I was thinking was, *Please don't let me have to see that guy again.* Regardless of the information he'd given me, feeling despair, being uncomfortable, and feeling a little overwhelmed came with his diagnosis. Those types of feelings were difficult to get rid of. For me, they persisted later in life, too. In fact, they showed up again in another doctor's office.

A couple of years later, my parents moved to another state, and once again it was time to get a physical. What was it with those doctors? After my last experience, I dreaded it. In fact, I can remember the exact weight he told me after I stepped on the scale. Even after all these years, I can remember the number because it was tied to all those yucky feelings. Did you know that yucky feelings carry *a lot* of weight? One hundred and sixty-seven pounds of yuck, to be exact. I was so upset; I came out of the doctor's office and cried. My sisters were thin and weighed in the lower one hundreds. I felt out of place and weird, like I was an anomaly.

I kept hearing the phrase *"big-boned"* from my coaches and others. I didn't know what big-boned meant. I thought I looked like someone who had the same size bones everyone else had. To me, "big-boned" felt like an excuse to be fat. After all, aren't all skeletons the same size? The weight diagnosis was heartbreaking; I just wanted to be normal without some doctor commenting about my weight. Little did I know that the weight comments would continue after I graduated high school.

During my college years, all my friends loved going out on Friday nights, drinking at the local bars. Drinking wasn't my favorite thing to do, but I loved hanging out with my friends. One night we were out, a fight broke out at the bar. You know, the typical fight between two males: I've had too much to drink and I'm going to show you how big and bad I am. As we were leaving, I looked over at this guy and said something to him. I don't recall exactly what it was, but I distinctly remember him looking at me and saying, "Why don't you just shut up, fat bitch?" I stood there staring at him and thought, *Am I really a fat bitch?* Now, I know we aren't supposed to allow others to define who we are, but in that instant, I totally took on the identity given to me by a guy I didn't even know. He was just some drunk dude who had no class. To this day, I ask myself why, and who calls someone that? Mean, drunk people with no class. That's who.

I wish I could say that being called a fat bitch made me want to make some changes. Honestly, though, all it did was cause me to sink further into my poor eating habits. College was where I learned that no one was watching what I ate. I could go to the cafeteria's hamburger stand every day at lunch if I wanted to. Ranch dressing? Yes, please, smothered over those hot, fresh French fries. There were no boundaries. In college, I went hog wild and ate all kinds of food. After all, there wasn't a parent telling me I couldn't have something. Do you want a giant package of Oreos at two in the morning? Yeah, baby. Let me show you where I keep them in my dorm room.

Finally, during my senior year, I realized I needed to get my act together. My university didn't have an established place to exercise, so I started visiting a local gym. I wasn't the typical gym rat, and the gym wasn't anything spectacular. It had a few machines, but the reason it appealed to me was that someone would design a work-out routine specifically for me. I usually didn't have a problem going to the gym as long as I didn't have to *think* about it. So, there I would be, three to four times a week working out.

A bunch of basketball players worked out at my gym as well. There were many days I was at the gym and saw one of the trainers, who would spend his entire time talking to the other girls. I thought to myself, *I must be invisible*. This was the first time I'd experienced feeling as though my size made me invisible. Oftentimes when you're heavy, you feel that even though you may be in a packed room, you're viewed by others as being so insig-nificant that you might as well be invisible.

But I kept going to the gym because it was my senior year of college, and I'd be looking for a job soon. I had majored in physical education. It may seem ironic; I knew what I needed to do to be healthy, but having that knowledge and actually acting on it aren't the same thing. Who would want to hire an overweight PE teacher? How hypocritical would that be? "Yes, please hire me for a job, even though I'm overweight and probably can't run to the end of the gym if I tried." Thankfully, the short time I spent at the gym yielded some great results. Well, that and the fact that McDonald's and I finally broke up!

Each of us has a time when we first become aware of our weight or when we are forced to step up and do something about our weight. Maybe it's that we compare ourselves to others. I've even heard stories of family members that are brutal to each other about one or the other's weight. For those of you being attacked by your own family, I am so sorry you're going through that. We all have battles of the bulge that we must face individually. It doesn't make my battle any easier or less than yours. It just means we fight it differently.

Starting points can be hard to deal with and to determine. I'm fairly sure you can remember the first time your weight being a problem was noticed. The great news is that our past experiences don't have to control our futures. Even though I'm blessed with my dad's stature and didn't grow up owning a scale, I persevered. You can, too. We must not look at our pasts and say, "I must stay here." The warrior says, "Because of these instances, I can learn and improve." You have the power to use the past to your advantage by learning from it.

*You* get to be the author of your own story.

# Adventure #2:

## First Comes Career, Second Comes Marriage

---

**M**Y FIRST TEACHING JOB was in the middle of nowhere in super-hot, desert-like California. I was thinner than I'd been in quite some time. I made the move to California on my own, with no family in the vicinity. It was a time of firsts for me: first apartment, first bills to pay, etc. I was so excited to be on my own. There was no one telling me what to eat, no curfew, no pressure to get to the gym—it was the same recipe for disaster, just a little later in my life. You'd think that after experiencing the ups and downs of weight loss and gain, I would have learned how to combat the pattern. But I hadn't. Instead, I tried to eat my way through the new experience.

One of my favorite things to snack on was raw, uncooked brownie dough or cake mix. I would take that happy, little, red Betty Crocker box and mix the ingredients just like it said on the back. Then I would put it into the fridge, turning the batter thicker, like frosting. Yum! Who doesn't love thick cake frosting? I'd indulge in this snack at least once a week. After all, cake mix cost less than a dollar, and I was living on a first-year teacher's salary.

Fruits and vegetables weren't staples of my diet. I would *maybe* have a can of peas or green beans once a week or so. My favorite dinner to make was Hamburger Helper or Tuna Helper. All those cheap items were what I could afford with a first-year teacher's salary. The problem was that none of them were healthy. But being healthy wasn't my top priority at the time. I was trying to survive my first year as a teacher, and I was trying to get used to being away from my family. I still didn't own a scale, and after the trauma I'd experienced at the doctor's office, I certainly wasn't going to buy one. Who would want to be reminded of their weight on a daily basis? Certainly not me.

As my career took off, my eating habits didn't change. In fact, when I started dating my husband, he would often ask, "What are you eating?" To his credit, he was raised on a healthy diet and typically had a salad of some type at every meal. While he ate his share of junk, he was stick thin and could get away with it. Everything I ate, on the other hand, made me heavier.

Following the weight gain were the obviously ill-fitting clothes. I looked like a giant sausage that had been wedged into a pair of two-sizes-too-small jeans—the ones you have to lie on your bed and suck in your stomach just to get zipped up. And after you pull them on, you jump up and look in the mirror and say, "Yeah, they fit"—when obviously they don't since now all that extra weight is protruding from every place it shouldn't. Instead of losing weight to better fit into the clothes I owned, I did the next best thing: I bought bigger, baggier clothes. I don't know if I thought all that fabric hid my larger form, but it didn't. Instead of acknowledging that I was actually buying larger clothes, I remained in denial. After all, if I wedged myself into a pair of large sweats, didn't that mean I was almost a size medium (even though I should clearly have been wearing an extra large based on how tight those pants were)? These were the types of mind games I would play with myself. I would pretend I was losing weight or getting smaller when in reality, my clothes were just getting bigger.

About five years into my career, my husband and I had been dating for a while, and it was time for our relationship to move forward. He was going to propose. He wanted the experience to be perfect, so he picked Sequoia National Park for the setting. What an awesome, romantic place to propose! The problem was that I detested any and all forms of exercise, and for him to be able to propose in the way he'd imagined, I needed to hike on this little trail.

I did not want to hike anywhere. I didn't even want to get out of the car. Having to get out and actually move threw me into a grumpy state, but I was finally convinced to hike up this minor trail. I'm sure it wasn't his idea of a dream proposal, as I had to sit on a log and rest multiple times on the way up so I didn't pass out. There I was, red-faced, cranky, and sweaty, as he got down on one knee and proposed. Sounds dreamy, doesn't it? Every man wants Grumpy Girl for a wife. But he certainly must have, because there we were, engaged!

It might seem logical that with the proposal acceptance, I'd be one of those brides who dreams of being thin and begins working hard toward weight loss so I'd look good on my wedding day. But this wasn't the case for me. I kept my same habits. One day I tried to ride my bike up this teeny, tiny hill to get some exercise. I had to stop and rest halfway to the top, which was probably three hundred feet at the most. I can't even imagine how that looked to any passersby—a fat chick *pushing* her bike up a hill. Doing that five-minute bike ride (well . . . rest and ride) meant I deserved some nachos grande slathered in cheese and guacamole from my favorite fast-food joint, right?

I was in such a sad state. I couldn't ride my bicycle up a hill, and I could barely walk to the end of the street without needing to rest. That whole exercise idea lasted about as long as that bike ride.

I, like all other brides-to-be, wanted the perfect wedding dress. I saw all those gorgeous gowns in the bridal magazines and wanted one for myself. What I didn't realize was those designer gowns weren't created for people my size. I wouldn't come to this realization until the first day I went dress shopping. As if bridal stress weren't enough, I had to sift through a billion wedding dresses all stacked in rows that weren't wide enough for my butt to walk down.

Shopping for a wedding dress at a place like Kleinfeld's definitely wasn't in my budget. The local discount dress store was more realistic for me, financially. One problem with discount wedding stores is they only keep dresses in smaller sizes in stock and have to order larger sizes. So there I am in a store with only a slim selection of sample-sized dresses. Imagine, if you will, a size-22 woman trying to wedge her body into a size-8 wedding dress.

In the dressing room, the attendant said, "Use your imagination and think what it will look like in your size." I have a pretty good imagination, but it's not *that* good. You can't look at a dress that's half as big as it needs to be and imagine how it will look on a body shaped like a big barrel. Not only was the dress too small, but I was shoved inside of it to the hilt, wearing a corset to keep my boobs and stomach where they were supposed to be. Then the attendant said, "Go out and show your friends and family." *Riiiiggghhhttt!* You want me to walk out in a dress that barely fit over my hips and pretend it looks good.

Isn't that how all the Disney princess brides look in the movies? The princess stands in front of her family with her complete back showing, her boobs barely tucked in, and excess boobage spilling out the sides. Oh, wait . . . that's not how they look. But that's how it looked for me. I wanted to sit in the parking lot and cry.

Shopping for a wedding dress was supposed to be fun. It wasn't. Because of the dress trauma that I encountered, one would think this would provide great incentive to start my weight-loss journey. Isn't that what brides say? "I went on XYZ diet to make sure I could fit in my wedding dress." Not me. C'mon, junk food, late-night nachos, and any other comfort food I could find. After all, this wedding planning stuff was stressful!

I needed a much more elaborate reason to lose weight.

Each of us finds the right time to enter our weight-loss journey. For me, there were many opportunities where I could have made the choice to lose weight. Sometimes the journey begins because of an upcoming special event. Sometimes because we can't fit into our clothes or we can't walk more than fifty feet without becoming out of breath. All of these would have been great reasons for me to make a change in my life.

But, no. The reason I decided to lose weight had to do with an almost unbelievable experience I had with my dad.

# Adventure #3:
## The Shorts Episode

---

WHERE WERE YOU when you finally made the choice to get rid of that pesky fat? Was it because of something someone said? Because of a diagnosis? Because of a demand made by a doctor or family member? Not for me. My reason was much more obvious than my clothes fitting too tightly.

One of the great benefits of being a teacher is the time off in the summer. During summer vacations, my now-husband and I would head to Montana to spend quality time with my family. I enjoy fishing and boating—the types of outdoor activities that help me appreciate nature. However, one summer, enjoying nature with my dad was an eye-opening experience I will never forget.

My Uncle Ralph has a super-speedy boat. In their younger years, my aunt, uncle, and dad spent their summer glory days waterskiing. On this particular day we were visiting during my summer vacation, my dad and uncle thought it would be fun to relive the old times and go out on the boat to play in the water with my husband and me. We were in the middle of the lake, laughing and splashing, when my uncle proposed water-skiing. In his glory days, my dad was a fantastic water-skier. My uncle goaded him into displaying his prowess and hopping into the water.

The problem was that my dad didn't have any water-ski shorts. Being a generally nice person, I said, "Hey, Dad, I brought some shorts to wear over my swimsuit; if you want, you can wear those." I was thinking, Here's a fifty-something-year-old, redheaded, Santa-shaped guy who will probably be able to just shimmy into my shorts—maybe have to unbutton them a little. I figured as long as he didn't lose them in the bottom of the lake, life was groovy. It was a good theory . . . until he began to pull them on.

My Santa-looking dad, who I love greatly, was standing at the front of the boat, sliding my shorts up his legs. Then the defining moment happened: he buttoned and zipped the shorts without any effort. Holy crap! I just sat, staring at him. The angels might as well have begun singing from heaven. All I could think was, *That must be exactly how I look.* A redheaded, Santa-bellied person with boobs. Sounds appealing, right?

It was one of those slack-jawed experiences. Surreal, unbelievable. I didn't say anything, but a million thoughts crowded my head. I stared at my father for a long time. There he stood, like a gladiator in my khaki shorts, all proud and saying, "Thanks, Suz. I needed some shorts." There I sat, dismayed. How could anyone think after witnessing her dad fitting perfectly into her clothes? It was a moment that would be forever burned into my mind. There isn't an eraser big enough to wipe away the image of my Dad fitting into my "little" khaki shorts.

As my fiancée and I drove home, we talked about my dad and the shorts. I was still in shock. The image of what I had to look like in those same "little" shorts simply wouldn't leave my head. I needed to do something, but what? Was there a super-fast-lose-eight-billion-pounds-in-ten-minutes diet book? If so, I needed it immediately. I could no longer escape that I had gained way too much weight. The skinny girl in me was buried so far down that I was sure she feared she'd never see the light of day.

We all have times in our lives when we decided enough was enough. We come to a breaking point where some act, word, or idea makes us decide we have to do something differently. In my case, it was the shorts, but in others' experiences, it could be a doctor's diagnosis. It could be that they lose a loved one to an obesity-related disease, or they could experience some other life-altering reality that shakes their worlds. Whatever the reason, each of us has to embrace it completely.

We can choose to fight against the truth or hide our heads in the sand, but neither of these options did a darn thing to change the fact that I was fat and needed to make some drastic changes. I call this my "why." The reason I chose to finally do something about my weight was my dad's age; he was in his fifties. I was in my thirties, and I had a choice to make. I could continue down the path to become heavier and able to do less, or I could take action. I didn't want to be a woman in her fifties who had two hundred pounds to lose and who wished she had done something about it two decades earlier.

There were many smaller "whys" in my larger reason for wanting to change. I was embarrassed. I was creeping up on a size-22 pair of pants—well, on the days I didn't try to wedge myself into a size 16 or 18, pretending I was smaller than I was. You know what I'm talking about. I called them my Empire State Building pants. As in, I had to jump into them from the Empire State Building for them to fit. Then, when I was zipped up in the too-small pants, I admired myself in the mirror from all angles, saying, "Damn, I look gooood." But it was a false reality.

I was lucky I didn't have any significant health issues like diabetes, high blood pressure, etc., but it was clear to me that it was only a matter of time before I received a diagnosis. I had youth and good health still on my side, but the degenerative disease clock was ticking. My why truly was that I'd had enough. There was no getting heavier for me. I had to decide: now or never. My why was enormous, probably about as big as those shorts into which both my dad and I could fit.

Whatever your why is, it has to be *huge*! It has to be so great that nothing can derail you. On the days you want to give up, your why has to be there, urging you on. When that bucket of ice cream is calling your name, your why has to drag your head out of the freezer. When raw brownie dough was yelling from inside the fridge, my why had to be like a giant pair of noise-cancelling headphones, making it so I couldn't hear my name being called. Your why—your willpower to make a change— must be enormous.

The great news is that each of us has a fantastic why. Our whys are the reasons we get up in the morning. They are the reasons we work out. They are the super-stars that dig us out of the doldrums, making us stand up and say, "Today, I am a warrior. I get to call the shots!" Be the person who says, "My why is what I live for." When your journey becomes difficult, dig deep and reflect upon your why.

You can even place reminders of your why around your home. Mine is written on my bathroom mirror. I see it every day, and it reminds me that *I am a warrior*!

# Adventure #4:
## Dreams Do Come True

LIFE-ALTERING DECISIONS can occur at any time and place. We're all just one step away from making a life-changing decision. Do we usually go searching to make these choices? I don't. But oftentimes we make small decisions that, when we look back, we think, *Dang! That was a huge moment!*

For example, one day I was sitting at my desk, sifting through mail. It was the usual stuff—ads for the local craft store, bills, junk—and then there was a postcard. On this nondescript white postcard was typed, "Run/Walk a Marathon." Run a marathon? Who does that? I couldn't even run to the end of the sidewalk. There was a bunch of dates for meetings listed on the back of the card, which you could attend to find out about the program. I will admit, running a marathon appealed to this little desire in me to do something big. If there's one obvious characteristic I have, it's that I'm not afraid to try something new. I am not afraid to fail, and if I do, at least I will have had fun in the process.

*Hmm? Is running a marathon really something I should try?* I showed the postcard to my husband and told him I was thinking of participating. He looked at me with total skepticism and said, "Sure you are." To be honest, when that postcard arrived, my marriage wasn't in the greatest of places. I was fat and miserable. We hadn't been married very long, maybe six years. We argued a lot, saying all kinds of mean things to each other. Spending time together was like nails scratching on a chalkboard: unpleasant—and no one wants to be around that. My life was at a place where I had to do something to improve it, or I had to get out of my marriage. I was slowly dying a miserable death with each day that passed. Deciding to go to a meeting about a marathon was one small decision that altered both my marriage and my life.

The day of the meeting, my husband and I had one of the biggest arguments we'd ever had. I was upset that he didn't believe I could actually run or walk a marathon—that he didn't believe in *me*. Isn't your husband supposed to cheer you on when you try new things?

Looking back, I realize, why *would* he have thought it was a good idea? I didn't do any sort of exercise. I was at the heaviest I'd ever been—in the 250-pound range. My idea of exercise was walking from the car to my apartment door. Why would he have thought I could finish a marathon? I certainly hadn't shown any signs that I could achieve that goal. Fortunately, or unfortunately sometimes,

I'm as stubborn and hardheaded as they come. The lot had been cast. If I'm told I can't do something, I will do all I can to prove that person wrong.

A few days following the initial meeting, I went to orientation to run/walk with Team in Training, a nonprofit organization that teaches individuals across the nation how to run/walk marathons, participate in triathlons, and go on amazing bike rides. It also raises awareness and money for blood cancers such as leukemia and lymphoma; in fact, the organization is the fundraising arm of the Leukemia and Lymphoma Society. Team in Training does unbelievable work, while helping a lot of people to go from being couch potatoes to athletes.

As I sat through orientation, I thought to myself, *This is it! This is the "something big" I can do.* I could choose to sign up for either a half marathon (13.1 miles) or a full (26.2 miles). Team in Training would provide all the support and training I'd need to get to the finish line. I was all in. I practically ran over people to reach the desk so I could sign up. My self-doubt reared its little head as I began to walk away from the registration desk. I couldn't commit to a full marathon, so I opted to sign up for the half marathon.

Team in Training's coaches were present so interested parties could ask questions. I needed to know that they'd properly prepare me for taking on a feat of this nature. After all, walking or running over thirteen miles is no small feat. I approached one of the coaches—let's call him Coach No—and asked if I would really be able to run a half marathon. He asked how far I could currently run, and I was honest: "About to the end of the street."

Coach No stopped for a second, looked at me and all my 256 pounds, and said, "Maybe you should meet the walking coaches," as he pointed across the room. In my head, the negative voices said, *He doesn't think you can do it.* Do fat girls not run marathons? I felt that obstinate, fierce girl starting to dig in her heels inside me. *Oh no, you didn't just say I can't run a marathon! I'll show you I can!* Thank you, Coach No!

I walked a little dejectedly to meet with the walking coaches, Ron and Cindy, a bit perturbed and a lot discouraged about running the half marathon. But the two friendly faces I encountered were a huge encouragement on that day and have continued to be so in my life. Sweet Cindy reassured me in her nicest voice, "Of course you can do it!" She became the long-lost beacon of hope for which I'd been searching.

Little did I know the impact Ron and Cindy would have on my life. They were the light I needed to start my journey toward weight loss and good health. I'm incredibly thankful for them and for Team in Training. *[Side note: If you ever want an opportunity to do something big and change others' lives, there are many charity organizations that can help you make an impact. Team in Training is a great one.]*

About two weeks after orientation, we had our first practice. I didn't know what to wear. What do you wear while marathon training? There certainly weren't any cute, frilly outfits suited for this big, 250-pound body. Trying to fit into small running shorts was out because— let's face it—no one wanted to see my flab hanging out! I was truly concerned that I wouldn't be able to find anything but a giant plastic sack to wear. I didn't want to be one of "those women" who wedged themselves into spandex that society makes fun of regularly. But then it was like someone was pointing at me, saying, "Newsflash, Suzanne! You already *are* one of 'those women.'" I had to escape the denial realm that insisted I was already thin and say to myself, "It doesn't matter what you're wearing as long as you're out there exercising." That's not an easy place to be. Facing the fact that clothes don't fit and people are more than likely going to judge you is hard! But I had to start somewhere—even if it was the inside of my closet.

## WARRIOR TIP

I've noticed that for some reason, I—along with possibly you or people you know—think I need to look a certain way in order to exercise. I'm pretty darn sure that appearance is the main reason women are hesitant to go to the gym, exercise classes, etc. They're concerned that other people will talk about what they're wearing or how they look on the treadmill. It doesn't matter. The very fact that you got up and went to the gym or to do whatever exercise you enjoy makes you amazing! Who cares if you had to wear a tent from Omar the Tentmaker's store to go to the gym (which, by the way, is what I'm pretty sure I resembled in my workout clothes). You are already a warrior because you made yourself a priority. Let the judgment of others go. Only your opinion matters!

That first day of training, Ron and Cindy said, "Today we're only going to walk four miles." Now when a person tells you this, and you've never trained for an event this big, you don't realize that at some point later on, you'll be ecstatic that it was *only* four miles. Those four miles weren't *super* hard, but it wasn't a cake walk for this fat chick.

Training for an endurance event takes a lot of time and energy. During the week, my husband and I would get up at five each day and walk the required distance (as determined by Team in Training). On the weekends, the entire group of walking and running participants would meet to walk our miles together. Sometimes the distance would be long, and sometimes it would be short. Regardless of how many miles we walked, the camaraderie I gained exercising with that group was awesome. Not only did I have my own personal cheer squad, but I had people relying on me to show up. That expectation was why I rarely missed walking on a weekend day. Joining a group exercise class is another great way to build a similar camaraderie with others who are working toward the same thing: becoming more fit! The more people in your group, all striving for a common goal, the more encouraging the environment becomes.

During one training session, I received a small piece of advice. I was talking with Coach Cindy about my miles of training and my plans for the future with regards to marathons and half marathons. We spoke about weight, walking, and diet—the usual conversation topics women address. My big question was: "When am I going to notice a change in my size?" After all, that was one of the main reasons I'd joined Team in Training: to lose weight. I was doing all this exercise, more than I'd ever done in my life. But I wasn't seeing the major results I wanted to see. It seems that weight loss never happens as fast as you want it to happen—as in, I wanted to be skinnier yesterday!

Interestingly, Cindy gave me some of the best advice. She said, "At some point, I hope you'll stop worrying about your weight and be happy with where you are." I wasn't sure what she was talking about, so I just politely told her that I would. I didn't quite grasp the concept of

Cindy's advice until much later in my weight-loss journey. Often we receive nuggets of information that we may not use right away, but later in life, that advice becomes invaluable. Pay attention to those little pieces of advice you're given. Later in life, your life could depend on that knowledge.

As I progressed in the training process, I became stronger and could walk longer distances without getting out of breath. I dreamed to run a marathon instead of walk one, but I hadn't really expressed that to anyone.

I was telling one of the other participants about Coach No and how he'd convinced me I couldn't run. It just so happened that Cindy was nearby. She sat down and began talking to me about being a runner. She explained that anyone could be a runner if they wanted, and she encouraged me to try a little running the next time we were out training.

The very next week, I was toward the end of a training walk, and the terrain was downhill for the last mile. I thought to myself, *What the heck! I might as well try. I have nothing to lose.* So I started to run down the hill. Okay, let's face it: It wasn't running. I call it the fat-chick shuffle. Those chubby legs weren't running anywhere, but they were at least moving faster than they had in the last decade. I felt free! With a giant smile on my face, I thought, *Take that, Coach No! I can run thanks to Coaches YES, Ron and Cindy.* Thanks to the encouragement from the YES coaches, I was able to make a small dream happen!

## WARRIOR TIP

Who encourages you and acts as your support system? We all need one. If you don't have support, find some! Reach out and find someone who has your back and your best interests at heart.

Facing the real reasons you do things isn't easy. Having to admit to others that you have a problem is sometimes more difficult than admitting it to yourself.

We were about twelve weeks into our training cycle, and a seventy-two-year-old woman named Jo was just cruising along next to me. She was so strong and vibrant. We were talking about why we were each doing marathons. Jo told me about her inspiration for walking: a young person who had leukemia and who had touched her life. It was incredibly moving.

Imagine: she had just told me this heartfelt, touching story. Then she looked at me and said, "What's your reason for joining Team in Training?" It took me a minute to decide what to say. I could make up some big flamboozled story about a youngster in my life, or I could tell the truth. It was confession time.

I looked over at Jo and said, "You want the truth? I'm tired of being fat." It was the first time I'd had to admit to someone that my reason for joining was my weight.

Admitting to myself and to others that I was fat was *hard*! It was almost as if I thought if I didn't acknowledge the truth, it would somehow not be true. But how could I hide that my clothes didn't fit? That my face looked like a giant tomato? Or that I was trying to fit into a XXXL sweatshirt? You simply can't hide that. No amount of fabric will hide that your body won't fit into a size small, and it was time to do something about it.

I wish I had an inspiring story like Jo's, but when I started the training process, it was all about me. I *needed* something to get me moving. I *needed* to prove to myself that I could accomplish something big. I *needed* to show the world that I wasn't just some "fat bitch" who had nothing going for her.

After I answered Jo's question, she just looked over at me and said, "I think that's a great reason. Oh, and by the way, I don't think you're fat."

I love Jo. She is an amazing lady, and I hope when I'm seventy-two I can still do marathons. During our walk that day, she made me realize it was okay to admit my shortcomings to the world. She even made it seem okay that I was struggling with my weight. She was exactly the person I needed to confess this to in order to be okay with the fact that I was fat and I was working on it. After all, you can't really hide your size, regardless of how much you want to deny it. Believe me, I tried!

Shortly after my awesome chat with Jo, I made the decision that I would walk a full marathon instead of a half. This could be the only time in my life I'd do a marathon or half. So, I figured, if I'm only going to do it once, I may as well do the whole thing. After all, "go big or go home" was my motto.

As I progressed and was able to walk and jog more miles each week, I noticed that I felt stronger. My body was walking more miles than it ever had before. The day of the marathon was quickly approaching, and I had just completed a double-digit training walk—more than ten miles. Imagine me, the woman who wouldn't walk to the end of the block, putting in double-digit training!

My husband and I were headed somewhere in the car, discussing the marathon. Now, cars typically aren't the best places to have deep conversations because no one can leave. So this talk was either going to go well or really badly.

I wanted to express to my husband how important it was for me to have his full and complete support. I needed to know that someone was on my side. I needed someone to believe in me. On the days I felt I couldn't walk one more step, I needed someone to say, "Keep going!" Even though I was doing all the training, it seemed as if my beloved was waiting for the next shoe to drop and for me to call it quits. I don't believe I've ever been a quitter, but I can see why he would think I'd quit.

After all, 26.2 miles is a long way for someone who just weeks ago didn't want to walk to the end of the street. Even so, the lack of support had upset me to the point that I had to say something.

So we were driving down the freeway and calmly having this long, deep discussion about how he was supposed to be my biggest fan. At that moment, enlightenment happened. A giant light bulb came on for him and for us as a couple. He realized I wasn't going to quit and that he could either choose to support me or not. I don't know if I can properly articulate the monumental change that occurred that day.

When I started training, my marriage wasn't in the greatest of spots. I was lonely, and I'm sure he was, too. No one wants to be married and lonely. At the time, he wasn't a big believer in words of encouragement. In fact, I would venture to say that he was the major voice of negativity in my life—along with my own negative self-talk. I certainly didn't need both of us saying mean things to me! And I didn't say the nicest things to him, either.

Whether at home or in public, neither of us could praise or encourage the other. It would always be the same old conversations: "Blame you for this. . . . You don't do this right. . . . Why don't you do XYZ?" We were cruel, damaging each other.

Marathon training made a *huge* difference in our relationship. We spent hours walking together in the early mornings. We only had each other to talk to, and this opened doors for constructive, positive communication to happen. There was something about the time—five in the morning—that made us try to be nicer. Maybe we weren't fully awake yet. Maybe it was because it was dark outside. Or maybe it was because for once we were forced to face that it would take both of us working on our marriage to make it work.

You see, joining Team in Training didn't just change me. It transformed my life. The training allowed for not only an opportunity to get healthier, but also for me to have difficult but necessary conversations with my husband, which forever changed our marriage.

After that important marriage-altering day, I often heard participants on my walk team say, "Wow. Your husband is the greatest. He's so supportive." Suddenly, he would show up to help the other walkers and runners when he previously hadn't cared. He would act as a water stop for the participants. He would make sure there was enough water and food for training walks. It was like I had a whole new husband. As my team members made comments about how great he was, I would just smile and nod.

We had finally turned that corner. I'm grateful that we were able to take a difficult moment and turn it into something that has helped us, even to this day. Those conversations changed our marriage and both of our lives. Who knows where we'd be without them?

The most important point of this story is that sometimes the people in your corner may not know what you need. They see you making changes in your life, and let's be honest: Change is scary. Friends and family members only know that you're becoming someone different. Different isn't always bad. But to the rest of the world, it can be intimidating or even threatening. People don't know how to deal with change, so they may not know how to deal with you. They don't know what to do to help you. They may not even know what you're up to. Be patient with them. Don't be afraid to ask for help; maybe they're waiting for you to make the first move. Maybe it will be like my experience and completely change your relationships. By not speaking up, you're keeping others from being a part of your fantastic journey. It's important to allow others' positivity in on your fun. Look around and determine who gets to join in.

## WARRIOR TIP

As your inner warrior starts to show up, the rest of the world may get a little nervous. The new warrior in you stands up for herself and screams, "Notice me! I am important." Let her scream, but keep in mind that your friends and family may be wearing ear plugs to squelch the noise. That's okay. Through your actions, they'll slowly start to see you as the rockstar you are. It may take time for them to embrace it, so in the meanwhile, keep moving! You never know who is watching you and who you are influencing.

What happens when you spend hours, days, and months training for an endurance event and then suddenly you've completed it and it's over? You're lost—at least, I was. It was as though I'd had a giant letdown. I had walked my first marathon in seven hours and three minutes. I'd had grand visions of all the weight I would lose. I mean, isn't that what happens in our fantasies? We start training for something, and by the time we're finished we're a size 2. In reality, I wasn't even close to the amount of weight that I had hoped to lose. Was one hundred pounds too much to ask for? Apparently so.

On top of all that, I still had the desire to be a runner, and I'd only walked the marathon. I was new to the exercise world, and my home was a little bit of a distance to train with Ron and Cindy. It was time to find someone in my area. I'd been doing the fat-chick shuffle on and off for a few weeks, and I wanted to exercise more intensely without causing myself injury. I asked around and discovered that some running-shoe stores host running groups, and some employ coaches. *Bingo!*

The coach's name was Doug, and he was the coolest guy. He was a veteran with one ankle that didn't have much movement at all, and his running gait wasn't common. But Doug—who's a triathlete, runner, and running coach—was the best thing that could have happened to my running dreams. As a way of giving back to the running community, Doug held Saturday-morning classes at a local park. Doug wasn't the type of person who tried running super fast, Olympic-mile times. He was, however, all about enjoying running with new people and teaching newbies like me how to run a 5K.

My couch-potato-loving husband decided to stop taking a back seat to my training and actually joined me on my newest expedition of becoming a runner. We would meet with Doug once a week, and he'd map out a plan for us. My goal was to successfully run a 5K in ten weeks. I wanted to get to the finish of a 5K without passing out or dying, which was a huge feat for someone who hadn't been a runner before now. Remember those high school mile runs? Hated those! So this was a big challenge for me.

Each week we would run the same path, and Doug would patiently see how much farther I could run, not jog, than the previous week. For a couple of weeks, it didn't seem that I was making any progress. There I was, huffing and puffing with a red face, trying to make it just one whole mile without succumbing to a lack of oxygen. I certainly wasn't getting any faster, and I most definitely wasn't able to run any farther. My husband, however, made great strides. He was like a calm, cool, professional athlete, making it look super easy. Not hard for a six-foot-two-inch daddy longlegs. Then there was me: walking a bunch because I was too winded to run, trying to breathe, and struggling to complete one running mile. It wasn't getting any easier, and I was becoming discouraged!

About four weeks into the ten week training, my husband could almost run the whole 5K. To see him making progress while I made very little progress was dispiriting. After all, it had been *my* big idea to learn how to run.

Then, it was as though a fairy godmother waved a magic wand and I gained a magic power overnight. I had an epiphany and decided I'd try my own running theory. *[Side note: Sometimes I try following through with theories and they pay off. Other times, they don't. But I figured I had nothing to lose by trying!]* I went out for a run and slow-jog, or my new speed, "fat-chick shuffle", as far as I could. Now, I couldn't have gone much slower without just walking, but in my world, my new speed was working for me.

On my own, I "fat-chick shuffled" the weekday miles Doug had provided for us, and suddenly, I could shuffle *really* far. If I slowed down, I could continue for much longer, and I wasn't sucking every ounce of oxygen I could from the universe by the time I finished.

The next Saturday, I showed up for the prescribed running routine. Poor Doug. I'm sure he was thinking,

*Great. Here we go again.* I explained my new theory of "fat-chick shuffling", and he started to run (well, I don't know if it could be called a run) next to me. We almost completed all three miles in one shot. He was shell-shocked and told me he was amazed. He had coached a bunch of runners in his time, and he said he learned something from me. No one had ever taught him that *you didn't have to go fast to go far*.

Learning to slow down was such a huge "aha" moment for both of us. I learned that I could run! Yay me! Doug learned that not every way of coaching works for everyone. Win-win! Discovering that I could run three miles was gigantic. It boosted my self-confidence—I had become a *runner*! My stepping stone was almost complete.

It was time to run my first 5K. I was strangely afraid that during the 3.1 miles the course would run out of water while I was out shuffling. To combat that fear, I loaded up my hydration belt with enough water for probably ten people. There I was, this fat chick wearing pants (because I didn't want anyone to see my fat legs), running with a hydration belt loaded with four water bottles—each holding twelve ounces of water—for a 5K that takes me about forty-five minutes to run. So, rest assured if you and I are ever on the same course, I will have plenty of water for both of us! To this day, every time I see the picture of me, loaded to the hilt with water, running that 5K, I laugh.

Even though I wasn't fast by any stretch of the imagination, it was all right because I had become something I had wanted to be: a runner!

## WARRIOR TIP

Weight loss results don't happen by making a hundred changes at once. If there was one thing I learned during this experience, it was that if I wanted to reach my goal, I had to break it into smaller chunks. Sometimes a chunk would be to make one change and achieve one goal before moving on. For example, at the beginning of my journey, I switched from white to brown rice. That was a big change for me. I had grown up on Minute Rice, out of the box. The next change I made was exercising three days a week. Now that didn't mean I'd do two hundred sit-ups or anything. I was merely going to put on my tennis shoes and go for a thirty-minute walk.

Great results are not achieved by doing everything at once. Great results are achieved by changing one thing at a time. Try something small. When you master that change, move onto another small goal. It also gives you the confidence to reach for another achievement.

When I started my journey, I thought I had to change everything at once. That's what I saw on TV. Isn't that what *The Biggest Loser* and the rest of those shows seem to be all about? But what I learned and what I want others to understand is it doesn't have to be like that. You can still achieve results by mastering one small change at a time. After all, we want this weight to be lost forever. This isn't some short-term goal. Slow and steady wins the race.

# Adventure #5:

## Poop or Get off the Pot

---

AVE YOU EVER met someone who wasn't even trying but still left a lasting impression on you? Sometimes impactful moments happen when you least expect them. My husband and I attended a taping of my all-time favorite game show, *The Price is Right*. I grew up watching it religiously every day with my grandma. I love Bob Barker, and getting to see a taping of that show has always stood out as an amazing experience for me.

In order to see a taping, you have to arrive early, way before the butt crack of dawn. Then you wait in a series of enormously long lines to get a ticket to *possibly* be in the audience. It's a long day, so you inevitably meet a lot of people, because what else do you have to do in line but talk to those around you? These people waiting in line next to you become your new best friends; you spend hours with them.

Hearing other people's stories has always interested me. I'm sure my mom was worried about me when I was a kid because I would talk to anyone. There are some

— 39 —

things I just have to know, even if I need to ask about it to find out. Curious minds need to know stuff, and I'm curious. Being curious leads to people telling me great stories. Win-win!

On this particular day, the ticket people offered my husband and me the option of attending a later taping. We figured, "Since we're already here, why not?" We walked to the local farmers market to have breakfast and noticed the couple who had been in front of us in line were also eating. We started up a conversation with them, sharing stories about our families and professions. You know, the usual small talk.

Then the woman, whose name was Kathy, began to talk about how she had lost fifty pounds. I was completely blown away. She was so calm about it, and the way she spoke made me believe that losing a large amount of weight was completely doable. I questioned her, asking how she had lost it and how much exercise she'd done. I was expecting her to answer that she had consumed only grapefruit and water and had been exercising the daylights out of herself. But she explained that she had joined Weight Watchers, changed her eating habits, and ridden her bicycle a few days each week. I was enthralled; I needed more information. Maybe this was finally the breakthrough I needed to get rid of my excess weight. Her story began the thought process in my mind that maybe it was possible to become thinner.

On our drive home, my husband and I had another deep conversation. I told him that I planned to do what the lady had done, and I wanted to look into Weight Watchers. My husband listened politely and then said, "I don't care what you do, but whatever it is, stick with it." As supportive as he was, he was tired of seeing me upset over my weight. He wanted me to be happy with my body, and to be successful with whatever I tried.

I went home that night and researched Weight Watchers on my computer. I didn't know anything about the program, but if Kathy could do it and make it sound so easy, then it was possible for me to do it as well.

## 🪶 WARRIOR TIP 🪶

You never know who you'll meet and what type of impact a person will have on your life. I truly believe in divine intervention and believe it's what made my path cross with Kathy. After we left *The Price Is Right* that day, we continued to communicate with the couple, but then they were hit by Hurricane Ike, and we lost communication. I would love to see her again someday and tell her she was my inspiration. Because of her, I saw that it might be possible for me to lose weight if I actually worked on my diet and exercising at the same time.

That encounter leads me to ask the questions: Who are you listening to? Are they making an impact on your life? Are they giving you ideas and hints regarding what and who you could be? Is the warrior within you trying to find the next best step? Are you listening to those who inspire you to move? If not, you should pay attention; by doing so, it could be the start of the most significant change of your lifetime.

You know the age-old adage, when life hands you lemons, make lemon cake? Okay, maybe that's not quite it, but honestly, what other choice do we have? When faced with decisions in life, we really only have two options. As my grandma used to say, you can either: A.) Poop, or B.) Get off the pot. I decided it was time to get off the pot.

Shortly after discussing Weight Watchers with my husband, I found the nearest Weight Watchers group and when they'd be meeting next. The first time I attended a meeting, I just visited and observed. I wanted to be certain this really was "the place." You know, the place that helps you lose a billion pounds? Yeah, that one. That was the place I was looking for. I needed to find somewhere I felt comfortable and with people and a program that would help me lose weight. What I expected to find in that first meeting was a bunch of skinny people who needed to lose only five pounds or so. What I actually found was completely different.

The reality was there were all different types of people in that room. Some were very heavy like me, and others only wanted to lose a few pounds. At the time, I thought, *What do those skinny-minis really know about losing weight?* It was such a judgmental place to be. I didn't know their histories. For all that I knew, they'd lost a great amount of weight and were simply further along in reaching their goals.

Each and every one of us who is on a weight-loss journey is in a different place. We who want to change are all sizes, shapes, and weights. I feel as if we're all chasing some elusive number that we believe we should weigh. I definitely had a number I chased, and I certainly wasn't happy with where I was. So did those skinny-minis have something to teach me? *Absolutely!* We can all learn from each other. We all struggle with weight issues in one *giant* conglomeration like Jell-O. No one's weight struggle is better or worse than another's. We are in it together.

By the week following that first meeting, I had made up my mind to join Weight Watchers. I got up very early on a Saturday morning and went to my nearest Weight Watchers center. I filled out all the paperwork, and then it was time to step on the scale. You know—the object I still didn't own. While I stood there in my stocking feet, I debated whether to get on or stay off that scale. "Wait!" I wanted to yell. "Let me take off every single possible piece of clothing I can before I step on that dreaded device!" I gingerly took my first step onto the scale. *[Side note: Why do we do that? We slowly step onto a scale as though we'll break it. Watch yourself the next time you step on the scale. Chances are, you do it too.]* The nice little reception-ist discreetly opened my weight-tracking book and wrote the number inside of it. She handed it back to me with a smile but without saying a word. I looked around for a seat, refusing to open the book and see my number. It was one of the few times in my life that I was truly ner-vous and uncertain about my weight. I didn't even want to see what that horrible, magical number was.

*If I open it, do I have to confront the number? Does this make it real?* These thoughts traveled through my head. The meeting began with the leader doing all of these cel-ebrations. *What? Celebrate? Who does that?* But all of us weight-loss hopefuls clapped and cheered for those who had lost weight during the week. We were celebrating their five-pound milestones. I wondered if someday that would be me everyone was celebrating.

At the end of the meeting, I got into my car and slowly peeked at that unhappy number. *HOLY COW!* Facing your demons sucks! As I drove away, I began to cry. I was embarrassed that I now weighed 243 pounds. All the months of difficult marathon training I'd just completed, all the weeks of learning how to run, and I'd only lost thirteen pounds. Thirteen lousy pounds. I know I should have been happy that I had lost any weight at all, but I felt like a failure. Who puts in five months' worth of strenuous training and only loses thirteen pounds? Even though I had made some positive changes in my life, it wasn't working out like I'd planned.

I had become so overweight that I honestly felt I was running out of options. I was still fat and unhappy with my weight, as I was at the beginning of my journey—only now I could walk really far. If there were ever a time I needed guidance, it was at that point in my life. I needed another divine intervention. I needed someone to show me it was going to be okay. *Please, Lord, give me something.*

Then she showed up.

During the first meeting, the leader had talked about the Weight Watchers website. She said there were recipes and ideas available there. The next day, I looked it up. On the website's home page, short stories scrolled across the top, written by people who had lost weight with Weight Watchers. The stories were incredibly diverse: people who were looking to lose small amounts of weight, and those hoping to lose large amounts.

Then, it happened. A story popped up about a woman who was overweight, lonely, and didn't know where to turn for help. She described how she had felt so desperate for guidance that she went into her bedroom, got down on her knees, and prayed to God for the knowledge and wisdom to lose weight. Her story was so much like mine that someone might as well have stepped out of that web page, pointed straight at me, and said, "YOU!" She described in perfect detail how I felt. I thought, *She's me. I feel just like she does. Maybe I should pray about the answer, too. Maybe it will help me like it helped her.*

I immediately stood from my computer desk, walked into my bedroom, dropped to my knees, and began praying. As I prayed, the same thought kept occurring to me: *I need strength that is greater than my own.* I needed not only God's strength—I needed His courage and His wisdom as well. Clearly, trying to take my weight-loss journey on my own wasn't working. After all, divine intervention had led me to Weight Watchers to start with. I surely needed God's guidance now. So I prayed fervently for help. I needed the right Weight Watchers leader and the right plan to help me move forward in my journey. I prayed for every ounce of help I could get: strength, guidance, wisdom, leadership— you name it, I prayed for it. I was desperate! But out of desperation comes opportunity.

One of my first prayers was answered when I found out I could attend any Weight Watchers meeting that I wished to. I wasn't a big fan of weighing in at night. Who wanted to drink a gallon of water all day and then step on the scale at nighttime, praying that the number would be smaller? Certainly not me. I had enough weight issues without adding water-drinking weight to my problems. So I shopped around for different meetings. *Eight in the morning on Tuesdays? Nope. I have to work. Noon on Fridays?*

*Nope, that won't work either.* The meeting I finally settled on was at seven on Saturday mornings. Perfect! Not a lot of people to fight for the scale, and I'd still have most of the day left to run errands.

Each meeting has its own flavor. Some meetings are more serious than others. I didn't know what I would find when I went to that seven o'clock meeting. It was very important to me that the leader and I mesh. If we didn't, I would keep shopping. If I was going to get up every Saturday morning and have to face the scale, I wanted to be sure the person cheering me on made me feel comfortable about it.

I met the most amazing, funny, brilliant leader that one could pray for. Her name is Kim. How can I describe the awesomeness of Kim? She's passionate about Weight Watchers, losing weight, and becoming healthier. She only wants the very best for every person she works with, and when you lose weight at her meetings, Kim is there with her bright-orange pompoms, dancing a little jig. I had no idea that Kim would be the best weight-loss cheerleader I could ever have imagined. Good thing God had planned it all.

The next Saturday, it was time to face the music again. I gathered up my courage and stepped onto the scale. Just like the previous week, I was afraid to look at the number, but I looked anyway, and this time, it was smaller. My weight was down about two pounds. *Only two whole pounds. Why wasn't it ten pounds? After all, I'd given up my favorite brownie mix for a week.* Two pounds in the scheme of one hundred pounds seemed like pennies in money terms. Of course it's great any time you lose weight. But in reality, all I could focus on was how far I still had to go.

For the remainder of the meeting, all I could focus on was that number. I got into my car after the meeting, and history repeated itself. I drove back home in tears. *Who cries two weeks in a row? Me. That's who.* I admit it: Frustrations and expectations sometimes get the best of me.

The entire task of losing weight was daunting to me. It was like I was facing all my evil demons at one time: fat chick having to lose weight and going for a giant goal. *That is scary!* But my fear wasn't that I would fail to lose an immense amount of weight. I wasn't even scared to take on this big, important challenge. The most difficult aspect was that I was forced to finally face the fact that I was fat. As I was about to step onto the scale for the third week in a row, the feeling that came over me was as though I was standing in front of twenty people and saying, "Hi. My name is Suzanne, and I'm addicted to chocolate." It was *hard*.

Having to own up to the fact that I had eaten myself into the position I was in sucked. I felt like a big, fat loser—literally. Confronting these feelings was difficult. It wasn't as though anyone gave me a handbook that said,

"At the beginning of your weight-loss journey, don't be surprised if you break out into horrible amounts of tears due to loserhood." No one told me that. No one gave me a road map. There were no warning labels, although it should have come with one reading: *WARNING! Total emotional rollercoaster will commence in five, four, three. . . .*

There are a lot of feelings that come with starting your weight-loss journey. Happiness, excitement, fear, and nervousness are all common. And let's not forget *stress*! If anyone ever says weight loss is easy, they're lying. I don't care what those lose-weight-fast midnight info-mercials say. It ain't easy.

Don't be afraid of your feelings. Don't think that just because you're riding an emotional rollercoaster, there's something wrong with you. I believe that any time you embark on a new adventure—whether it's a new career, a new house, a new relationship, etc.—all the aforementioned emotions are a normal part of the process. Why would weight loss be any different? The fact of the matter is . . . it isn't.

But—and this is a big one—a time will come that we have to put on our "big-girl panties" (in some cases, literally), be brave, and step forward. Don't be afraid of whatever feelings may come next. Don't quit on yourself or convince yourself it will be "too hard" or any such nonsense. Just accept that you're going through something new and different, and it's all going to be okay. I guarantee that if you embrace the journey on which you are about to embark, it will seem a whole lot more fun and exciting. How about if today, you make a giant note to yourself that says, "Today, I am putting on my big-girl panties and embracing the new journey I am about to take. Even though it may difficult and scary, I'm going to take a chance on the possibility of a brand-new me." This opens the door for a world of opportunities—even if you at first feel uncertain. Wear your big-girl panties with pride, and then get ready to buy smaller ones!

## WARRIOR TIP

All diets are not created equal. When I started Weight Watchers, I decided I wouldn't do the point-counting, which is essentially counting calories. The alternate plan at the time was a list of foods you could eat all you wanted of, as long as you stopped when you felt satisfied. Having a list of foods to eat not only helped at home with meal planning, but it also helped me make better choices when I ate away from home. By following this type of plan, I was forced to track exactly what I ate (which was something I'd never done before) without having to worry about how many ounces, pounds, cups, or calories were involved. All I had to do was to focus on when to stop eating. Instead of stopping when I felt full, I had to stop when I felt satisfied—not too full, not too hungry. I always hated the feeling of being full. You know what I'm talking about—when you've eaten to the point that you have to unbuckle your pants because they're so tight, or you wear your favorite pair of sweatpants so you won't have that tight feeling . . . that kind of full. I hate that feeling.

My Weight Watchers leader frequently talked about "catching your sigh." The theory was, if I listened to my body while eating, I would eventually experience that "I'm satisfied" type of sigh. When I did, I had to stop eating and just rest. I would find that I was at the perfect point—not too full, but no longer hungry. The sigh is the optimal spot to reach.

Before I learned about the sigh, I would wait until I was incredibly hungry before eating. Then I would eat everything that wasn't tacked down and would be super full, and the cycle would start all over again.

Between the food-list plan and learning how to catch my sigh, I knew what I was allowed to eat and when to stop. This is what I used for my weight loss, and it's a technique I still use today and recommend highly.

# Adventure #6:

## Apparently Failure Is an Option

---

I AM AN EXPERT self-saboteur. Are you? How long is it after you've started working toward your goal that you sabotage yourself? Is it a few days, weeks, months? For me, it was only a few short weeks before the dreaded chocolate attack happened. What I call "The Great Chocolate Incident" taught me that no matter what mistake I make, it's okay to laugh at myself and start over. I'm not perfect, and I don't ever expect myself to be. I'm human, and funny stuff happens to me. *All the time!*

I'd been participating in Weight Watchers for about a month, and I was having a tough week. When I say tough, I mean the stress was overwhelming me. It was the beginning of a new school year. I felt pressure to start the school year off right, so I began working long days to perfect my lesson plans. I was having some trouble staying focused and wanted so desperately to throw in the towel. All the common elements—stress, fatigue, anxiety—were stacking up. My allowing those factors to stack up caused me to sabotage myself. When I become stressed, chocolate calls my name. Okay, "calling my name" might be putting it nicely. Chocolate *screams* my name from the depths of its box.

I looked into my pantry, and there it was, like a light beaming: the bright-red box of Betty Crocker brownie mix. I couldn't withstand the temptation. I thought, *I'll just make the mix and eat a little bit of it. It'll only be a little bit. I've made it these last few weeks without cheating. I must have this chocolate thing beat, right? I can surely have just a little bit and survive the big temptation.*

I was so wrong. I grabbed that box, threw in all the ingredients, mixed it up, and then I let the spoon-licking commence. The ultimate, chocolate, rich, thick, gooey goodness was just flying down my throat. One lick turned into one spoonful, which turned into one cup. I tried to put it back in the fridge. I thought I was finished with it.

*See that! I defeated temptation. I only ate a cup!* Wrong! About three or four hours later, I had that bright-blue bowl out, and the wooden spoon and I were friends again. After about a day and a half, I had eaten the *entire* bowl of raw brownie mix. Uh-oh. The guilt set in. All the negative thoughts I knew so well began invading my mind. *What am I going to do? You're a loser. You can't do this. See, you can't resist temptation.* And then the ultimate blow . . . it was weigh-in day. Crud. What was I going to do? It wasn't like I could UN-eat the mix. I couldn't drop the weight in half a second. I couldn't eat enough celery to make up for that mix. I guessed I was going to have to weigh in. *Time to pay the piper. Crap, crap, crap!*

The scale and I had a big showdown. I didn't want to get onto it. I knew I had to face the consequences of eating so poorly, so I slowly stepped on the scale. My sweet, friendly Kim looked at the number and said in her kindest voice, "So, how did your week go? Anything you want to tell me?" I might as well have been in a church confessional.

I coyly said, "Well . . . I may have eaten an entire box of brownie mix."

She said, "Oh, after you cooked them?"

"Oh, no. They didn't make it into the oven."

She began to stare. "Oh," she said. "Did you get sick?" *Yeah, I got sick, all right. But it wasn't from the raw eggs like everyone's presuming.* Even in those short weeks, I had changed my eating habits. No longer could I eat that much sugar and not feel the effects it had on my digestive system. Did I get sick? Absolutely. I was incredibly sick from that sugar. Of course, it didn't stop me from eating the rest of the mix, but boy, I felt terrible afterward. *Welcome back, self-saboteur! You only made it through three weeks.*

After telling Kim about The Great Chocolate Incident, the weekly meeting began. Kim's topic for the week was temptations or something of that nature. She walked from one side of the room to the other, trying to be nonchalant. In her cute voice, she said, "So, does anyone want to share any temptations they've had?" She tried so hard to make it seem like an innocent question, but I knew exactly where she was headed. She may as well have taken a giant pointer stick, pointed to me, and said, "Suzanne . . . want to confess your soul?"

## WARRIOR TIP

Excuses or results? You can make excuses, or you can make results. You can't do both. You can't exercise your way out of a poor diet. Whatever it is that you want in life, you can only make one of two things happen: results or excuses. No one gets stronger at the gym by not going. Whatever is important to you, you *will* make time for it.

Think about your time as if it were a checkbook. Wherever you spend the most money (or time) is what is the most important to you. If you want to lose weight, you have to make the time to do so. Now, that doesn't mean you have to become a crazy lunatic and obsess about everything that goes into your mouth. In fact, if you do become like that, I can tell you it will only be short-lived. At one point in my journey, I decided I wasn't going to spend my life memorizing points, calories, or anything else. I wasn't going to be somebody so freaked out by her weight that she worries about everything that goes into her mouth. However, I *was* going to be mindful of what I ate—and I still am. I want to be healthier, and I know that when I eat a lot of junk food, sugar, or my favorite—chocolate—I don't feel my best. When I go for a run after I've spent time eating crappy food, my run goes terribly. My realization was that you can't feed your body *crap* and expect it to perform. It needs good fuel with a little indulgence now and then, not the other way around. Note to self: Sucking mud on a short three-mile run makes for a crappy and miserable day. Feed your body better!

After Kim asked the group if anyone had a run-in with temptation, I figured I might as well admit my relapse with the raw brownie mix. I raised my hand and told the group about my binge-brownie-mix attack. It was laughable to me as I spewed my confession.

All the women were staring at me. It was almost as if they couldn't believe I'd eaten it all. "Did you get sick?" they asked.

"Yep, sure did, but not from eggs," I said. Then, in a moment of hatefulness of which I'm not proud, I thought to myself, *Don't make judgments about me. You all didn't get to this meeting because you overindulged on carrots! You got here just like I did—eating Cheetos or cookies or whatever.* Not a single one of them verbally judged me, but the voices in my head believed they were internally criticizing me, just like I was doing to myself and to them.

The truth of the matter is that each one of us has a go-to food that we use to calm our nerves or as a pacifier for stressful times—or even when we're bored. I'm not alone in my chocolate addiction. You know what? It's okay to say it.

Hi! My name is Suzanne. I eat raw brownie mix.

There. I feel much better. At least I now recognize my comfort release food for what it is. I know that when I'm ready to grab a box of brownie mix out of the pantry, something else in my life is triggering that response. No matter how unhappy, sad, or frustrated I feel, no amount of brownie mix will take away those feelings.

It was in that moment at the meeting, owning up to what I had done, that I realized I couldn't eat my feelings away any longer. I needed to find a healthier way to deal with them, like going for a walk or calling a friend—anything I could do to get away from the pantry.

So often, we try to comfort ourselves with food. Maybe the food brings back a comforting memory, or the smell of the food itself is comforting to us. The problem is, it isn't the food that comforts us. *We comfort ourselves.* The sooner we face our triggers, the sooner we can move past them.

From this experience and many others, I've learned that when I'm tired or stressed, I crave sugar. If I hadn't stopped, paid the piper (so to speak), and owned up to The Great Chocolate Incident, I wouldn't have had the opportunity to face those feelings. How many times did I sit down and eat a whole box of raw brownie mix before realizing what my triggers are? Too many to count. How many more boxes would it take for me to realize I can't eat enough brownie mix to get rid of those feelings?

Out of this session of self-sabotage came the most amazing epiphany to add to my "eating lessons": It's okay to screw up. After I ate the brownie mix, I had all those icky feelings that accompany doing something wrong. I had messed up. I was working hard to be perfect and to reach my goal. If I was upset or having a bad day, I tried to eat my feelings away, and then when I was done, I felt horrible. Because the feeling didn't go away, I then felt bad because I'd broken my diet. After that, I thought, *Well, since I've already screwed up my diet, I might as well ruin it for the rest of the day.* Have you ever been in that cycle? It's a form of self-sabotage that I'm pretty darn good at. And after the sabotage is complete, I feel guilty and dumb—as though I'm not worthy of success. It's not an enjoyable place to be, nor is it comforting.

At another Weight Watchers meeting, one of the leaders talked about the vicious cycle that self-sabotage causes. She then gave me some fantastic advice that has stuck with me since. She said, "What would happen if you let it go? What if you just counted all those crappy foods as vegetables and moved on?"

What would that mean? What would that look like? What an amazing concept! If you count it as a vegetable and move on, there's no reason to beat yourself up over eating something "bad." There's no reason to continue the vicious cycle. You can say to yourself, "Yep, I screwed up. I'm not perfect. Now I can move on from it." There's no guilt or remorse. There's no reason to continue to eat everything else that isn't tacked down because you've acknowledged it and have reminded yourself that it's okay. There's a big difference in how that feels. If you know you screwed up and can move on from it, you experience the "whew, I'm normal" feeling. If you have guilt, remorse, sadness, and self-sabotage-inducing feelings, you walk away thinking, *I suck at this.* I'd rather concentrate on those good feelings.

There are going to be bumps, setbacks, and difficulties. Don't expect the road you're travelling to be smooth. It will likely be hard. But I promise that the rewards you receive will be worth it if you stick with it. This, too, shall pass, and your journey will be once again headed in the direction you wish. It's like that old saying that the end justifies the means. One day you'll look back and be thankful for how far you have come.

*It's okay to fail.* There are only winners in the game of weight loss. Of all the things that I hear, what grates my nerves the most is when I hear, "I was good and I ate. . . ." or "I was bad and I ate. . . ." Newsflash, everyone! Nowhere on a nutrition label is there a proclamation of "This is good food" or "This is bad food." There are foods that are less healthy than others, sure, but some people associate eating poorly with being bad. "Bad" brings on feelings of worthlessness, self-doubt, and self-criticism. Being "good" implies that we've eaten well and are happy and worthy. There should be no good or bad feelings connected with food.

When you eat something, you get to decide how you'll feel about it. Before I learned this concept, I would experience a lot of crappy feelings. I would feel like a failure or that I sucked at this weight-loss thing. You know what? We are worthwhile individuals regardless of what we eat. My worth and your worth are not defined by food. If you're going to eat something, after you're finished, just own it. Don't start the cycle of feeling bad, eating more poorly, feeling even worse, etc. This negative cycle can be stopped by simply saying, "Yep, I'm going to eat this. Yep, I'm going to have to work out harder to lose it. Yep, it's worth it to me." This takes away all the power we've given food. STOP! *Stop* the game of judging whether you're good or bad by evaluating what you eat. *You have the power!*

The caveat to this is that you can't count everything you eat as a vegetable and move on. If you do, then what was the point of the work you've done to come this far? The vegetable theory is about acknowledging our mistakes. It's the same with everything we do in life. We won't always be perfect parents, employees, students, etc. There will be times when you screw up. I do it all the time! *It's okay.* There is nothing that says we have to be perfect in all our endeavors. We're human!

Parts of the journey will be frustrating, and you'll likely face some weight setbacks. Maybe you'll eat a whole box of brownie mix. Maybe the cookie dough will call your name. Maybe that entire package of double-stuffed sandwich cookies will scream at you from the pantry. It's okay. One of the greatest lessons I learned on my weight-loss journey is that I'm not perfect—and you can't expect to be flawless all the time, either.

Admitting imperfection doesn't make us weaker beings. In fact, I believe that in times of imperfection, we experience the most growth. It's during those trying times that we learn who we are. It's during those times the brownie mix has temporarily defeated us that we can rejoice in the fact that it doesn't have to defeat us again and again.

For days on end prior to The Great Chocolate Incident, the brownie mix and I hadn't been friends. We'd pretty much forgotten each other's names. I needed to rejoice in that. What's keeping you from rejoicing? What do you need to release? After that release, what feelings will you have? Happy ones!

Sabotage comes in many forms. It can come from your-self or others. How many times in our lives have we sab-otaged ourselves? How many times have you given up on a goal because it was just too hard? Or what about the times you told yourself that you would start dieting, exercising, or avoiding chocolate tomorrow? How many times have you said to yourself, *I'll only cheat on myself this one time*? It happens to all of us—sometimes daily, some-times even hourly. We are often our own worst enemies.

I've self-sabotaged, and I still catch myself doing it. I tend to sabotage myself the most when I'm so close to reaching my goal that I can taste it. In the middle of my journey, my Weight Watchers leader, Kim, put together a hundred-day exercise challenge. We had to exercise for thirty minutes a day for one hundred days straight, and if we missed a day, we'd have to start all over again.

So, there I was on day one hundred. I had worked out for ninety-nine days in a row, and the finish line was in sight. I got up that morning and told myself that I had all day to get in those last thirty minutes. I'd made it ninety-nine days getting my exercising done early in the morning. But not that hundredth morning. That final thirty minutes was on my mind all day, and the pressure was weighing me down. I waited until eight o'clock that night to complete my last thirty minutes. Most people who had joined the challenge hadn't made it past the first week, and there I was, getting ready to sabotage myself at the last minute.

How many times have I done this? Quite a few. I believe that we all sabotage ourselves at some point, either consciously or subconsciously. I've noticed self-sabotage rear its head in my friends as they close in on achieving their goals. Is it the fear of failure or the fear of success? For me, it was both. When I got close to reaching my goal weight, I noticed that I'd occasionally do things to sabotage my goal: maybe a little snack here or a cookie there. But that saying, "The way you do one thing is the way you do everything," was very true. Not only had I self-sabotaged during my weight-loss journey, I'd done it on my exercise journey—and probably on a thousand other journeys as well. The good news is that now I'm better about recognizing my self-sabotage habits so I can put a stop to them, and you can be, too, if you pay attention.

Each step of my journey has included my learning an amazing lesson. There isn't a single journey I've gone on that I haven't ended up gaining or learning something by the end of it. At times, it will feel like you're at a standstill, like in a freeway traffic jam. During those times, take time to reflect upon where you are and how you got there. Are you sabotaging all the hard work you've done? Are you standing your ground and going out guns blazing, or are you standing back to let others shoot for you? All of the aforementioned are okay places to be, but it's important to recognize your self-sabotaging habits for what they are. That's what I had to do.

After I finished that thirty minutes on my hundredth day, I stopped and really thought about how many times I'd leaned toward self-sabotage when trying to achieve goals. It's giving up on something right when you're about to accomplish it. Don't vote yourself off the island before you've even had the chance to explore it. Who knows what you'll find if you allow yourself to discover a new way of being you?

## WARRIOR TIP

I see challenges and obstacles in life as opportunities to grow as an individual. A piece of coal becomes a diamond because of pressure. Pressure makes us grow. Sometimes as the opportunity presents itself, it may be difficult to navigate. It may be embarrassing. But all in all, every prospect we choose to say yes to will cause growth within us. We can learn from every experience to own up to our choices and actions—and we can decide to go a different route. What opportunities have you been trying to ignore because you'll have to face some ugly truths? What would happen if you jumped both feet into the challenges instead? Would it diminish the uncomfortable feelings that we try to eat away?

Go for it. If each of us gets comfortable being uncomfortable, we'll be presented with so many opportunities to better ourselves. This attitude will help us make the changes necessary to have the best pieces of us magnified and made greater. If you shine a diamond with a cloth, it becomes more brilliant. The same holds true to you—if you shine yourself by grasping and following through with opportunities, you'll shine more brilliantly. What opportunities are you missing? Will you choose to become comfortable with the uncomfortable—and take on those challenges?

# Adventure #7:
## Fat Chicks Do Go to the Gym

A s a way to become stronger, I embarked on a new adventure: going to the gym. Newsflash! Fat chicks can go to the gym, too! I have experienced and witnessed negative attitudes at the gym relaying verbal and nonverbal cues that fat chicks are not welcome. There have been at least a few times that I've heard gym-goers, both male and female, criticize or be mean to heavier women. The judgment from others kept me—and I'm sure others—from wanting to go to the gym. Before I became brave, I had witnessed during the few times I went to a regular gym that they were "meat markets"—it seemed that men were there to hit on women or to find their next date. There was a whole lot of standing around and exchanging phone numbers instead of any actual exercising taking place. The thought of putting myself into that type of perceived negative environment kept me from joining and sticking to utilizing a regular gym.

I started out with a Curves for Women gym. No men attended, and I didn't have to worry about being judged because of my size. I attended Curves for quite some time and then graduated to a larger chain gym. It wasn't an easy transition. I wanted to stretch myself a little by trying new classes. I couldn't find those at Curves, so I had to "graduate" to a traditional gym that offered all types of classes.

Any time I've tried a new exercise or class, it has sucked. One time I thought I'd go to a Pilates class. My big fat body was trying to make this Hula-Hoop do something amazing. *What? You want me to take that Hula-Hoop and put it around my feet and do sit-ups? I can barely do sit-ups without a Hula-Hoop!* It was a terrible experience. I didn't go back to that class—but it didn't stop me from going to the gym. I kept trying classes until I finally found one I liked: spinning. The reason I love it so much is I can set the gear on whichever one feels difficult for me. No one knows what my speed is or what gear I'm in. I like that I can go hard at my speed and the guy next to me can pedal like he's training for an Ironman. We can be in the same class and both get a good workout.

Since we're talking about gyms, let's talk reality. My friend told me once that when she went to the gym, she was intimidated just by being there because she felt like she didn't fit in. I thought I was the only one who was intimidated by the gym. As I progressed further into my weight-loss journey, I hired a trainer to help me become stronger. I'd been lifting weights with him for a little while when he said, "Why don't we graduate to free weights?" He may as well have said, "Let's go lift a thousand pounds."

If you regularly go to the gym, you know exactly who goes in the free-weight area. It certainly didn't seem like it was meant for overweight people like me. It was for those big, buff dudes who lift a ton of weight. I was incredibly intimidated. My trainer, Jereme, just sat there, staring at me. He couldn't believe I was so scared. We walked around that free-weight room as though I belonged. I'm thankful that he pushed me. It was an incredible experience—and scary at the same time. But I know that at some point, I need to put on my big-girl panties and face experiences that scare me. I guess that day was the time for me to face one of my fears.

You belong at the gym just as much as the next person. You pay the same amount of money as those big, buff guys. One day in the late afternoon, I was working on a lat-pull machine at the gym. This guy walked up and said, "Excuse me, why are you working on that machine?"

I looked over at him and said, "Excuse me?" I mean, I hadn't been talking to anyone. I'd been minding my own business, doing my exercises. I was just trying to get in and get out of there. This dude frazzled me. I couldn't articulate why I was working on that machine because I felt like everyone was staring at me, waiting for an answer. AWKWARD! I looked at him, and no proper words would come to my mouth. He began to try to explain how to focus on a different muscle group using the lat-pull. I so didn't care. What I wanted to say was, "Could you just leave me alone?" Instead, I made up some muscle I was working on, got up, and moved. I experienced a mix of emotions. I was angry because I'd only wanted to be left alone to work out. Working out in the free-weight area was scary enough without some random guy talking to me about it. I'm sure he had great intentions and was trying to help me, but in my mind, he wasn't helping one bit. Instead, he had embarrassed me.

I wish I could say that only happened to me once. Another time, I was sitting on the bench doing triceps dips. You know, the kind where you lift yourself up off the bench? Some guy said, "Oh, that weight's heavy. Do you want me to help you lift it?" I wanted to scream, "How do you think this weight got here!?"

The more that I frequented the gym's free weight area, the more "help" I got. I had to come up with a plan to remedy this situation because quitting wasn't an option. What concerns me about these types of experiences is that for some women, this would have been enough of a reason to quit going to the gym. Don't be one of those women.

My solution was to go to the gym early in the morning. It seemed less of a "meat market" at five in the morning than when I went at five in the evening. One tip I learned is to wear my headphones, even if I'm not listening to music. Without my headphones on, some male always wants to talk. Some well-intentioned gym-goer feels as though he needs to give me advice.

Don't let anyone intimidate you from improving your life. You have the right to be wherever you want to be—including the gym. Own the space you're in. Fat chicks can go to the gym, too, and we *do* know how to use weights! Rock your gym!

Judgment happens wherever you are: the gym, work, and maybe even at home. I am not proud to admit that I passed judgment on others when I first joined Weight Watchers. A couple of times during my journey, I was judged, too, by people who took one look at me and made a mental decision about who I was. There were many times I might as well have been invisible.

For instance, my husband and I like to travel. We stopped at a running store while visiting a state in the Midwest. I was looking for shoes, running clothes, etc. My husband and I walked in together, and we both started looking around the store. The saleswoman looked over at me, then proceeded to walk toward my husband. He looked at me and said, "Are you invisible?" I said, "Apparently."

I find humor in it because I can sort of understand the judgment. He's over six feet tall, thin, with Daddy

Long Legs. People automatically assume he's the runner in the family. He does run, but when I ran my first marathon, people kept asking him why he wasn't out there running. He's fortunate: He can eat whatever he wants and not gain any weight. So of course he looks like a running athlete. I think it's incredibly unfortunate that people judge others based on their appearance. Just because I was heavy at the time didn't mean I couldn't complete a marathon. It also didn't mean I wasn't a runner. After all, slow is a speed. At the time, it made me think of the movie *Pretty Woman*. You know the part where the salesperson says, "We don't have anything here for you" to Julia Roberts? That's how I felt! Little did she know that I was a long-distance athlete.

Also on your journey, you'll come across doubters. Don't let them stop your progress. I can see how having someone doubt your abilities could cause you to doubt yourself—or give up entirely. Sometimes doubters are threatened by what you're accomplishing. The doubt they share isn't always about you. Sometimes it's because they see you making a change, and it causes some terrible insecurity they have to flare up. Don't feed or take on someone else's insecurities. I have friends whose families are sabotaging their weight-loss efforts. They make snide comments about my friends' weight loss—that they won't keep the weight off.

Judgment happens to runners, too. Someone tells a future runner they can't do a marathon or a 5K. Know that other people's doubts and judgments aren't about you. Just because family, friends, or salespeople doubt your ability doesn't mean you have to accept that doubt as your own. It also means that the goals you set out to achieve don't have to be about others, either. It's okay if you succeed without the acceptance of others. It isn't about them. It's about *you*. It took me a long time to learn it's okay to be who I am. Don't let it take you a long time to figure that out.

## WARRIOR TIP

Not everyone will be on your journey with you. There may be people who don't want to see you succeed. Maybe this saboteur is someone you love. Maybe it's someone with whom you work. Not everyone will know what to do with the new person you become. There are going to be times when someone tries to derail your success. Don't hold it against them. Most people don't do it intentionally or to be mean. They do it because they don't know what *to do* with the new you. They're scared of the person you're becoming, and the most natural reaction is to put you back into that familiar space you were in while you were heavy. They still love you. Be patient with them.

# Adventure #8:

## A Walk to Health

While we cruise on this important weight-loss journey, what do we use as milestones? Is it the amount of weight we lose? Or do we somehow define the progress made in another way? I used a few gauges to mark my weight-loss journey. Some were weight related, and others had nothing at all to do with weight.

After I ran my first 5K and walked a marathon, I felt stuck in a slump. I had completed my first marathon, and in my crazy wisdom, I'd discovered that I wanted to run another one. Was I becoming an exercise junkie? To me, those people bordered on the edge of crazy! But there I was, signing up for a second race. By coincidence, the race would be in nearby San Diego—the Rock 'n' Roll Marathon. I was up every morning at the crack of dawn, putting in crazy walking training *again*—and with a smile on my face. I was determined to be faster this time. I wasn't going to have all those crazy problems I'd gone through the first time, like blisters and fatigue. I would learn from all of that.

About five weeks before the marathon, my husband and I decided to try completing our training miles at a new location. We'd heard that a nearby lake had a great dirt path for running. As a bonus, we'd be out in nature instead of pounding the pavement in our local neighborhoods. We had been watching the weather, and it was supposed to be blazing hot—in-the-hundreds hot. There were warning signs posted about the heat, reminding us to hydrate. My husband and I had a plan that was supposed to keep us smart, safe, and hydrated. We would run out a quarter of the specified distance for the day and then return to the car to refill our water and get some food. Then we'd go back out a quarter of the distance in a different direction and finish up by running back to the car. Great plan! No need to carry extra water or anything. Well, sometimes great plans don't turn out as expected.

We were training for my husband's first marathon. We don't move at the same pace because of his daddy longlegs and my short legs. But I wasn't worried about either of us. We had *a plan*! (Well, until we didn't.) Off we started. There weren't many other people on the path; I was sure the heat had scared them away—or it should have. As I walked along, approaching the spot where we'd go back to the car, I decided I'd keep going. After all, I was feeling *good*. It was only four and a half miles back to the car. *I can do this!* My husband's type A personality caused him to stick to the plan, and he was already on his way back to the car. I, on the other hand, in my hardheadedness, was traveling along with not enough water or food to make the distance. But it wasn't too hot yet, so I figured I'd be okay—even though there were all those warning signs. I thought I knew better than those silly signs! If only I'd turned around when I was supposed to.

After I'd reached the turnaround point and was headed back toward the car, it became increasingly hot. There weren't any trees along the path, so the sun was beating down on me. It was nearing ninety degrees and I was out of water. I kept slowly trudging along. My walking became slower and slower, and I'm certain a snail could probably have moved faster than I was at that point. My feet were getting heavier. It was becoming difficult to keep moving.

I kept hoping someone would see me. I don't know who I thought would see me because the smart people were indoors! I came upon this little-bitty shade structure that had a couple of benches. I wanted to sit and rest for a long time. The problem was the temperature was so hot that no matter how long I sat, my body's temperature wouldn't lower. I figured, *If all I'm going to do is sit here and sweat, I might as well sweat while getting closer to the car.* I got up and continued to walk.

As I moved along, I spotted a porta-potty. It was hot, and the only thought crossing my mind was, *I just want to sit and rest.* It didn't matter that it might stink. It was hotter than blazes inside that little hut. Imagine: There I was inside a porta-potty, and I was starting to scare myself because I was hot, sweaty, and inside an even hotter structure that smelled! My thinking obviously wasn't very rational at that point.

I didn't know what to do, so I began praying as I walked down the path. "Please, God, just let me get back to the car," I prayed over and over again. I was starting to freak myself out, so I called one of my friends. I don't even know what I told her other than I was at the lake and it was hot. I must have sounded terrible because my dearest friend kept offering to come get me. She was so frightened that she made me keep talking to her. After I'd been talking to her for a few minutes, I told her I needed to hang up because I was struggling to walk and talk at the same time.

After I hung up, I suddenly felt a cool breeze cross my skin. There had been no breeze before. Was it the answer to my prayers? I thought maybe I was finally getting a break from the heat—except now I was beginning to shiver. I was in trouble and beginning to get scared. Finally I turned that last corner and it was as if the angels were singing in big, loud voices when I spotted the parking lot. I had never been so glad to see my car. The bigger concern now was that I was incredibly sick. I didn't know it at the time, but I'd given myself heat exhaustion. Sometimes stubbornness doesn't always pay off for me. My stubbornness had been paying off on my journey to be a better me, but it wasn't working in the "I know better than you" department.

A couple of days later, I still wasn't feeling well, so I made a doctor's appointment. I didn't have a regular doctor, so I'd called a sports clinic in my area. I figured that type of doctor should understand endurance athletes, right? After all, that's what a sports clinic is about (or so I thought)! When I got in to see the doctor, I began to explain how I'd become so sick. He just looked me up and down and said, "You know, people train for months for these types of endurance events."

What was he getting at? Did he think I'd just woken up that morning and decided to do a marathon? This wasn't my first rodeo. I'd been training for almost a year.

Have you ever talked to someone and felt like you were speaking to a brick wall because they'd already made up their mind? That's how I felt—that the doctor had made a judgment about me based on my appearance. I tried to explain that it wasn't my first marathon and that I'd been training for months. But I don't believe he ever looked past my size. He started talking to me about losing weight and how maybe I should try exercising. *HELLO! That's what I'm trying to do!*

Looking back, I'm sure he was just trying to protect himself—and me at the same time. But he didn't know anything about me, and he didn't *want* to learn about me. His advice was for me to drop out of the marathon for which I'd been training for months. He said what I was doing was detrimental to my health.

I sat in his little office and cried big, giant tears. I was having a hard time breathing from all the sobbing. My months of training felt like they'd become worthless. I felt defeated. I was exercising and doing the very thing doctors prescribe for obesity, and this doctor had just crushed all the hard work and time I'd put in. After careful consideration, I decided to follow his advice and stop training for that race. This incident was another chance for me to learn about myself and how strong I am. Although my hardheadedness had gotten me into that predicament, it was also my hardheadedness that reared up and said, "You don't get to dictate my future, Mr. Doctor."

The old me would have taken that doctor's advice and run for the hills, never to exercise again. I would have hidden in my room, licking my wounds, and would have given up on my goals and dreams. But the new me, well . . . she got pissed. She was tired of others making judgments about what "people like her" were supposed to do. You know what? "People like me" don't have to be super-fast athletes with less than 5 percent body fat. "People like me" are just as capable of completing a marathon with proper training as those fast athletes. I've seen "people like me" overcome a lot. Why? Because they are *awesome*!

## WARRIOR TIP

Before I ran my first marathon, I had a preconceived notion of who "those people who run those things" were. But in actuality, I learned that people of all shapes and sizes run and walk half and full marathons. The very fact that overweight men and women are willing to do some type of exercise regardless of their size is admirable. It doesn't matter if you finish at the back of the pack or the front of the pack. Why? Because the distance doesn't change no matter how long you're on the race course.

My heart rests with the back-of-the-pack runners and walkers. These people are on the race course for a much longer time than most of the other participants. This means that during summer races, they're out in the heat for a much longer time. They have to deal with the possibility that the finish line could be removed or the course could be closed before they're able to finish. They push themselves—*hard*—for a lot longer than the elite runners. Let's face it! Moving a large amount of body weight for a long period of time is *hard*. It's *strenuous*! The people at the back of the pack tell themselves, *I am going to finish this race. I am going to push my body and make it work hard because I AM A ROCKSTAR.*

Our bodies will do almost anything we ask (even inside of a porta-potty!). If you're afraid to try something because you don't think you can do it, you're wrong. Try everything that scares you. There are only limits if you believe in your limitations instead of your abilities. We become victorious when we break past our perceived limitations. Adversity can produce victory. How you claim that victory will determine what you achieve next.

So I'd decided not to move forward with the marathon, and I was at loose ends. I'd gone from exercising without changing my diet, to dieting without exercise because I still went to Weight Watchers every week. When I realized how stuck and frustrated I felt, I started searching for ways to stretch beyond my comfort zone. I was be-bopping to work one day when I heard an ad on the radio for the Susan G. Komen 3 Day®, which is a sixty-mile walk. This would be my next big thing. I'd already proven to myself that I could walk twenty-six miles, so what was an additional thirty-four? The 3 Day wasn't a timed event, thankfully, but it did feel like one giant, fun party on legs. Besides, if I couldn't walk that far, I could always catch a van to pick me up! The thought occurred to me that if I were going to put in all this effort to lose weight, then I would make an impact on others in the process. In my heart, I believe that every one of us has opportunities in life to help others. While we help others, we can also help ourselves. If we choose to capitalize on them, we create situations where everyone wins. I was already paying to attend Weight Watchers, so I figured I might as well get the most bang for my buck. And in the process, I'd help someone else. That made it a win-win situation!

I talked my dear friend Coach Cindy into signing up with me. What a great joy it was to get to walk with her. Not only did we have to walk dozens of miles, we also had to fundraise for our walk. The 3 Day was like no other event I'd witnessed. The spirit of the 3 Day is that of kindness, support, love, happiness, and a whole lot of walking. The camaraderie and support were almost unbelievable. I was deeply dedicated to the training for the 3 Day; every morning, I was up early, walking. I did double-digit miles on both weekend days. I wanted to be *committed* to my goal. I doubted myself many times, but my stubbornness held out. I didn't want to do the fundraising and training only to have to take a bus to the finish line because I couldn't walk the distance. Not that there was anything wrong with the people that did, but in my stubborn state, I didn't want that to be me if it didn't have to be. I didn't want to put in that much walking for such a little reward. I'd come a long way from wanting to slowly walk on a hike. How far I could walk was a gauge I used to measure my success. I now wanted to walk sixty miles. It had become clear that I could walk farther than I'd ever thought possible. Who was this new me?

The second gauge I used to mark the progress of my journey came via a fluke in the middle of training for the 3 Day. On a visit to my gynecologist's office, they confused me with another patient. To make sure the office didn't have my chart mixed up with someone else's, I requested a copy of my records. No big deal, right? I wasn't super worried about it, but I thought it was better to be safe than sorry. After I got home from work one evening, I saw a thick manila envelope on my desk. It had been a while since I requested my medical records, so I had completely forgotten about the request. I sat down at my desk and began to thumb through the records. I sorted them by time and looked through them for comments the doctor had made and results of various medical exams.

As I read, I noticed one page in particular that stood out. It shocked me so much that I stopped turning the pages and just stared at it. In my stupor, I must have made some kind of sound because my husband turned to look at me, asking if I was okay. I couldn't formulate words to express what I saw. In large capital letters written on the page were the words "MORBID OBESITY."

I didn't know what to say or think. Disbelief, along with a thousand other thoughts, ran through my head. It was as though I'd been hit with a rock. I couldn't turn the page, and I couldn't stop staring at those giant words. I'd had no idea it had been written in my chart, and I felt like a deer in headlights.

In the doctor's defense, I'm sure he was concerned about my weight. I was nearing the 250-pound mark, and it must not have seemed to him that I was working to get any slimmer. There is no doubt in my mind that morbid obesity was a big concern. But how do you get over the shock of seeing those deadly words on a page of your medical records? What was I supposed to do now that I knew? *Do I run and hide my head in the sand? Do I pretend I never saw that diagnosis?*

I continued reading my chart, but I couldn't get rid of those words. Morbid obesity. Morbid obesity. They were imprinted on my memory. After I finished looking through my records, I just sat there, dumbfounded. I told my husband that I couldn't believe it said that in my chart. I was thinking, *Does that mean I'm going to die? Does that mean if I don't lose all this weight that I won't make it? What exactly does "morbid obesity" mean?* My poor husband continued asking if I was okay. I replied that I *was not* okay. My emotions churned. My gut hurt. I felt like I needed to throw up or cry. Or both. I was angry and hurt and still shocked.

At that moment, I made a decision. I could either live or I could die. I would choose to live. It was a like a bur had found its way under my saddle. I jumped up, headed toward the bedroom, grabbed my favorite walking shoes, and went for a walk.

This is where my moment of victory came into play. Upon seeing those words, the old me would have reached into the fridge, found the nearest container of milk, retrieved my favorite sleeve of Oreos from the pantry, and had a giant cookies-and-milk picnic in front of the television. She would have indulged in the sadness and depression of it all. But the new me couldn't stand it. The new me chose to take ownership of her life. I didn't want to die from morbid obesity. I could choose me. I *was* choosing me! An aha moment—I didn't have to be stuck with a label someone else had given me. I could alter my label.

And just like that (ta-da!), I had created a new label for myself. Morbid obesity was a thing of the past. I didn't have to wear that label anymore. My new label was strong, powerful, and courageous. The new me chose to be successful.

Success is not always tied to a scale. Oftentimes we measure progress by a number. In society, numbers carry a lot of meaning. If we make more money, we're successful. If we close a certain number of deals, we're successful. But a person's worth and level of success aren't always defined by numbers. We can address and define our successes based on how *we* want to define it. We are *way* greater and *way* more successful than what we see on a scale. We have to be careful not to give power to a

---

scale. Celebrate each achievement by your own definition. Did you walk past the cookie jar without grabbing one? Success! Did you eat a handful of carrots instead of jelly beans? Success! Only you know what your success looks like. Don't allow a device or another person define your success.

Even though I had my "walk against morbid obesity," I won't lie—there were instances when scale victories were a big deal, too. I had set a goal to finally weigh under two hundred pounds by the first day of the 3 Day. I did everything I could to get to my goal. I probably hadn't been in the one-hundreds in years. I wasn't even sure what that number would look like on the scale.

The week before the 3 Day was to start, I weighed in. This time, no tears were allowed. Was 199 too much to ask? I mean, really, I'd been busting my butt for weeks. Was it too much to ask that I actually weigh in at the weight *I* wanted for once? I stepped onto the scale, and when the receptionist told me my weight, I jumped off, let out a huge yell, and did a little dance. I had been walking my butt off for weeks on end to reach that goal. It was a momentous occasion to finally be in ONEDERLAND! I couldn't believe I had finally reached one of my weight goals. I was now past the fifty-pounds-lost mark. Maybe reaching 160 pounds *was* achievable!

# WARRIOR TIP

Weight is okay. At some point, I had to decide that a certain weight was okay with me. In the middle of my weight-loss journey, I had a water submersion test done, which measured my muscle-to-fat ratio. The results from that particular test taught me a valuable lesson. On the BMI charts (which use height to determine how much a person should weigh), it said I should weigh 160 at the most. After the submersion test, I learned that at 160, I was at the correct muscle-to-fat ratio. I found that if I dropped under 155, it messed with my fat and caused amenorrhea (a loss of my period). All my life I'd been told I was muscular, but it wasn't until the submersion tests that I realized those big, muscular legs I'd inherited from Dad were okay to have. I had believed that I needed to look like some skinny TV model to view myself as thin. Lesson learned. Sometimes it really is okay to be heavier. If you ever have the chance to get a lean muscle water submersion test, consider it. I learned that the scale isn't always representative of what's happening inside the body.

# Adventure #9:

## Talk to Me

The week after the 3 Day was Thanksgiving. It was the first time in my journey that I'd have to deal with a major holiday and food. I had worked really hard to get into Onederland, and I didn't want to gain that weight back in a week.

How many family gatherings do you attend that are surrounded with food? I'm from the Midwest, and when we gather, it always involves food. Any time someone visits home, we gather to eat. Whenever there's a wedding, a funeral, or sometimes just because it's sunny out, we have food. Well, not really that last reason, but you get the gist. I call it the permanent potluck. The worst part of getting together for food is that you can't control what everyone brings. The best part is usually someone brings a well-loved, passed down from generation to generation recipe everyone loves. However, what one person considers healthy, another may not. For example, my dad claims, "Lettuce is for dipping in your ranch dressing." I happen to disagree! It can be a little difficult for people who haven't seen you in a while to adjust to the fact that now you don't eat the same foods you once did. It's perfectly normal. My food choices were different. I paid more attention to portion size, and there were some foods that I no longer even enjoyed.

I've had to work through the challenge of creating healthier alternatives for my favorite foods. After all, low-fat Oreos aren't quite the same as the double-stuffed ones. I had to remember that eating healthier was a life-style change. This wasn't just some fly-by-night fad I was adopting. I wanted to make a difference in my life. But, of course, there would be some stumbling along the way.

What happens when you stumble? What do you do to get back up? When I was struggling on the weight-loss plateau, there were many times I wanted to throw in the towel. To this day, when my eating habits get out of control, I have to work to get them back on track. The weight-loss journey isn't one where you arrive some-where and that's it. Think of it like you're on vacation. Once you reach your destination, it isn't as though you just stand in the street and say, "Yay, I'm here." No, if you want to travel, plan to do some sightseeing. The same holds true for a weight-loss journey. Once you've arrived at your goal weight, you don't say, "That's all, folks." No, you have to plan to maintain that weight.

Here is what I know to be true: The weight-loss jour-ney is a life-long one, at least for me. Maybe some people can lose the weight and never have to worry about it again, but that isn't true for me. Every day, I have to be mindful of what I put in my mouth and what my state of mind is when I eat. I'm not so lucky that I can eat whatever I want and call it good. Does it make me frustrated some days? Hell yes! Have I learned to keep working at it? Absolutely. No amount of Betty Crocker is worth completing the journey all over again. There are days I'm pissed that I have to work at maintaining my weight. There are days I'm thankful to be where I am.

I believe, no matter how hard it is, it's easier to get back up within the next five minutes and keep trying than it is to start all over a hundred pounds later. Only you can pick up where you left off and keep going. Sure, it would be easier if I could just sit down with my favorite Twix bars and have a grand old time. I'm sure they miss those times with me. But to me, the risk of a Twix session isn't worth possibly giving up the reward. The more you stay the course, the more you will see that. I want to be in control of my life. I don't want food to control my life. I'm guessing you feel the same way.

## WARRIOR TIP

Others' acceptance of your new lifestyle is part of the change game. I had to teach my family and friends that I didn't want to eat big, fat French fries any more. I wasn't going to eat an entire brownie sundae now. I knew how many miles I would have to run to burn those extra calories. But my friends and family weren't used to this new person.

That I was willing to avoid self-sabotage was a victory for me.

It would have been easy, especially during the holidays, to throw in the towel and say, "It's only one day." But the problem with allowing a Thanksgiving food tsunami is that quickly it turns into a Christmas food hurricane, and then a New Year's Eve food thunderstorm. Then a New Year's resolution will have to be made, when we could have avoided the tsunami and all that followed it. Notice that there aren't a ton of people running to weight-loss centers in November and December. But in January, look out! You will get *run over*! It's not easy to exchange holiday food for better choices. I chose to focus on the great times I had with my family and not on the tempting foods that were available.

When it seems that you won't reach your goal, look at both your small and large, non-scale victories as well as your scale victories. Any time you can feel successful about getting closer to your goal is a *giant victory* in my book. There were times I was super frustrated and it seemed it would take a decade for me to reach my weight goal. I had to stop and look back at how far I'd come. I certainly didn't gain all that weight in a week, or even a year or two. I couldn't expect to lose it that quickly, either, much to my chagrin. Be patient, and rejoice in the small steps!

If there were ever one thing I wish I could go back and change, it would be to enjoy the journey. I was impatient, wishing that the weight would come off already. I wish I had instead enjoyed the hard work and time it took to get the weight off. Those steps made me the person I am now. While in the process, it seemed long and arduous, but looking back, the beauty of the journey is arriving where you want to be. Arriving at your goal after you've come so far is the most special moment. It is the moment when the victory of what you have accomplished becomes apparent to you. If I could offer one piece of solid advice, it would be to enjoy the journey. You can never go back and do it again. Journal it. Take pictures. Document however you want because when you're finished, you'll want to be able to look back and say to yourself, "I am not going there again." Trust me!

One day, I was reading an article that outlined how to speak more positively to ourselves. How many of us do that type of self-talk? Sure, it's a whole lot easier to feed the negative voices in our head. Why? Most likely it's because we've done it for such a long time and it's become a habit. For the longest time, even when I had a success at the scale, I would look into the mirror and say something negative to myself. It seems crazy, but I would do it almost every time I looked into a mirror. I would verbally beat myself up, saying things like, "It was *only* two pounds that you lost" or "You don't look any different." Or, even more destructive, I'd say, "You can't do this!" This is terrible, self-defeating talk. It sucks! It doesn't accomplish anything, and it surely didn't help me.

One way the article listed to help defeat negative self-talk was to write a message on the bathroom mirror. That way, when I looked into the mirror, a positive message would be there. *Hmm. . . . Seems like a good thing to try.* I stopped reading and went into my bathroom. *What to write with? Oh, look! It's a really old lipstick that I should have thrown away 3 years ago!* So there I was, writing a love letter to myself on the bathroom mirror. The next morning, my husband got up, looked at it, and said, "What's this?" "Oh, that," I said. "Just a little note to myself."

A few weeks went by and my husband asked me, "Can I erase that message on the mirror?" "Sure!" He scrubbed and scrubbed. Apparently it takes a long time to get lipstick off a mirror. The next morning, there was a dry-erase marker sitting by my sink. Note to self: Don't use lipstick to write your positive mirror message.

Writing a note to myself every week has been a huge inspiration for me. This may seem like a minor idea, but it really does lift my spirits every morning when I'm fixing my hair. Who doesn't want to read a positive note?

Sometimes my husband will even write one. The messages change over time. Sometimes it will be my goal for the week. Sometimes it will just be a love note like, "I am a warrior." Or sometimes it will say, "I am sexy, skinny, and amazing." Why do I do it? Defeating self-talk doesn't get us anywhere near where we want to be. It holds us back from showing the world our awesomeness. These words are sometimes so strong that I repeat them throughout the day or even during the week, like a mantra. I can't stress enough what an important part this plays in my journey. Being good to ourselves on our weight-loss journeys can only help us feel good about who we are and who we're becoming. Why not write a reminder somewhere to celebrate each day?

When you reach a victory, it's perfectly okay to reward yourself. How many of us have said, "When I achieve this goal, I'm going to have (insert your favorite snack here)"? But doesn't that defeat your whole goal to lose weight? Try to find a reward you really want. Maybe you want to get your nails done. Maybe you want to purchase new clothes. Maybe you want to take a mini-vacation. Maybe your reward is you're going to hang out with your friends or see your favorite movie that was just released.

One of my favorite things is to get a pedicure. So I would set a goal that if I lost five pounds, I'd get a pedicure. The benefit was my little toes looked great, and I reached my goal. Don't set a goal so large that it's unachievable. Your goal could be that you'll work out three days this week. Or maybe it's that you'll skip dessert for five days this week. Goals don't always have to be weight related, but they can be. Pick a goal—either non-scale or scale—but make it doable.

# Adventure #10:
## A Journey of a Thousand Miles

A s I TRAVELED ALONG my journey, new pieces of me began to develop. There were times my husband looked at me and said he didn't know who I was anymore. I'm sure that was true. I was gaining more confidence in myself and in what I could accomplish. No longer did the unsure, unconfident girl exist in me as she had before. With this newfound confidence, I began to do things that I previously wouldn't have done.

One of the greatest hurdles in my life had nothing to do with weight. I was afraid to fly. It made me nervous and so anxious that I'd throw up. After I'd run a couple of marathons, I decided I wanted to run in Nashville, Tennessee. I love country music, and in my mind, there could be nothing better in the world than mixing my three loves: my husband, running, and country music. But I didn't have time to drive there. Flying was my only option. My husband booked the tickets. I pretended for months that I wasn't really going to fly. I mean, I knew we were going, but if I pretended we weren't, I wouldn't become anxious. As the day approached, I became more and more anxious. After we arrived at the airport and were getting ready to board, I was so nervous that I went into the bathroom and heaved my guts out. My husband was becoming anxious because he wasn't sure I'd go through with the flight. They called our boarding numbers, and I headed down the jetway. I got to the door opening, looked down at the gap between the jetway and the plane, and thought to myself, *All I have to do is like I've done before and just take one step.* My husband looked on as I took a giant step over the opening and went to find my seat.

You see, the experiences you have as you try to reach a goal may affect you in other areas of your life. When the label of morbid obesity showed up, I had to take one step. After I found the postcard to run a marathon, my training started with one step. Everything we do begins with just one step, the first one. It doesn't matter how far we go or how fast we go. It doesn't even matter in which direction we go. All that matters is that you take one step. That step leads to another step. When you're trying to achieve a new goal, if you take one step, you'll be one step closer to that goal than you were. The process of moving forward is what helps us achieve greatness. It's all about movement. It's when the movement stops that you have to worry.

The movement stopped for me about a year into my weight-loss journey. When I say stop, I actually mean a halt! As you travel on your journey, sometimes you'll think it will be easy. Why? Because maybe it has been up until this point. In my case, reaching my goals had been pretty easy for that first year after I'd gotten serious about diet and exercise . I was shedding some weight, and it wasn't super strenuous. That isn't to say that losing the weight was easy, but it does mean I wasn't miserable with my current weight.

## WARRIOR TIP

It may take some time for other people to notice your weight loss. It may be after you've lost a significant amount. I found it intriguing that it wasn't until I'd lost thirty pounds that my coworkers noticed I'd lost weight. I remember thinking, *Crud, how much weight do I have to lose before people notice?* It made me acutely aware that the amount of weight I needed to lose was so great that thirty pounds barely made a dent in how I looked.

When I got to the fifty-pound mark of weight loss, my friends and family started to wonder if I was sick. It's a good feeling when you're becoming thinner, but at the same time, it was a little disconcerting that people assumed I was ill. They thought maybe a sickness was why I'd "suddenly" lost weight, when in actuality it wasn't sudden at all. I reassured everyone that I felt just fine and I'd be okay.

But then the weight loss started to crawl. I'd been averaging a one- to two-pound loss per week, and that number was dropping. I had lost fifty pounds in six months. Then it felt like time was standing still. I was down to losing 0.5 or 0.2 pounds per week. What had happened? Why was it now in slow motion? What had I done wrong?

I had hit the dreaded plateau. My Weight Watchers leader, Kim, had talked about the plateau. She gave examples of people who had been on their plateaus for a month or so. When she'd talked about it, I had thought how great it was that I hadn't experienced it yet. At that time, I was almost in an arrogant place because I started to believe I wouldn't reach a plateau. I had this false sense of security.

For almost eight months, I'd weigh in and be down a pound; then the next week I'd be up a pound. The yo-yo cycle was so frustrating! My leader kept saying, "Hang in there. It's going to be okay." Then I would get frustrated and self-sabotage. It was a horrible, non-stop cycle.

When your goal weight seems incredibly far away or you're dealing with your own plateau, remember that the weight you are today *is someone's goal weight*. This still resonates with me now. When my weight is up and I get down, I think about how my current weight is a weight someone else hopes to reach. It helps me keep perspective, and it helps me be grateful. Above all else, if you're grateful for where you are, there's no place to go but up, right? Always be grateful for where you are because someone is wishing they were there.

One day, I decided to do something different. I met with my chiropractor, Dr. Shin. We had a long talk about what was keeping me on my plateau. The discussion that ensued concluded with the advice that I completely remove sugar and carbs from my diet, along with following a strict outline of exactly what to eat each day. When we sat down that day, Dr. Shin said, "Are you sure you're ready to do this? You can never go back to this place in your life again. You won't be the same person at the end of this six-week regimen." At the time, I didn't quite know what he meant, but I later learned that he was right. That piece of advice about never being able to go back to the old me has stuck with me. I can't ever go back to who I was because I am no longer her. I no longer do and see things the same way. When I get ready to try new exercises or set new goals, I now remember I can do anything!

Any time we make movement in our lives, it changes us. We can never be the person we are in the beginning that we are in the end. Although it's scary each time I try something new, I am always grateful for the experience. Who wants to stay in the same place their whole life?

When I started this new regimen, Dr. Shin asked about my goal weight. I answered with some number off the top of my head. He just stared at me. I couldn't imagine I'd hit that weight at the end of that six-week cycle. I now truly believe that during a goal-driven journey, when we state what our goal is and go for it, we will achieve it 100 percent of the time. As I traveled through those six weeks of strict dieting, I learned that I am way stronger than I ever believed. I am capable of being amazing. I was able to stick to the no-sugar rule, and along the way, I learned that I didn't know or recognize who I was becoming.

I had *finally* hit my goal weight during the regimen, but now what? Once you achieve the goal you've dreamed about forever, what do you do? What's your next goal? How do you maintain all the work you've done? I had been on that plateau for so long that I hadn't believed I could reach my goal weight. But I had.

I didn't know what to do next. I didn't even know where to turn for the answers. What happens when you become the skinny chick after having been the fat chick for so long? Do you suddenly recognize yourself as skinny? Can you see the person you've become? At what point do you call it quits and say, "This is it! I'm happy where I am"? I'd been chasing the magic number for so long that when I hit it, I had no idea what to do. In fact, I sat in the doctor's office and cried.

You'd think I would have been happy to finally reach my goal weight—that I would have done a giant dance of joy, but instead, I cried. I didn't know how to accept who I was and who I'd become. I was unsure of myself because instead of wishing the weight was gone, I worried now that I would gain it all back. I had worked long and hard to get that weight off, and now that it was gone, I was more confused than ever. I didn't want to celebrate my success because I was afraid it would vanish.

Because of this fear, I spent hours exercising and tracking the food I ate. If I didn't get an exercise in, I'd worry that the dreaded weight would return to the scale the next morning. I'd freak out if I missed a session of weight lifting. If I didn't go for a run, I would feel guilty, like I was letting someone down. I'll admit it: I was on the verge of being seriously obsessed about weight loss. It was pressing down on me like a yoke for oxen. There's nothing worse than feeling burdened by guilt or worry. I couldn't let it go. I would worry in the middle of the night. I would stress early in the morning.

It was a problem, to say the least. It took me a very long time to accept my weight loss and recognize myself as a thin woman.

# Adventure #11:

## Two Forks in the Road

---

One situation I had to face was that I was close to the golden age of thirty-five; I had to decide if I wanted to have children. I'm not going to sugarcoat this situation. I struggled internally with it for a long time. My husband and I hadn't been trying to have children, but we weren't consistently using birth control, either. It felt like if it happened, it did; and if not, okay. But as I got closer to my "golden age," when the doctor is telling me I have to start making decisions about children, the decision becomes inevitable.

Now that I'd finally gotten the weight off and was getting a little comfortable with my new weight, I had to decide if I wanted to put the weight back on to have a baby. I'm sure it's never easy to decide whether or not to become a parent, but compounded with the weight loss, it was extremely difficult for me.

At one point, I was at a friend's house, sitting on the patio. He and his wife had just adopted a son, and I could see the joy on my friend's face. While he and I talked, I kept staring at their family's interaction and wondering if becoming a parent was right for me. The internal debate must have been apparent because my friend looked over and asked me if everything was okay. How do you explain to someone that you're inwardly conflicted about whether or not to have kids? Is that something you just blurt out loud? I could see how happy they were and how much fun they were having. . . . Was that direction my life was supposed to take? Did I really want to gain my weight back?

In my circle of friends and acquaintances, and even at Weight Watchers, the biggest complaint from women is that they were thin until they had children. In a great commitment to raise children, oftentimes women put their health and weight loss on the back burner. I know it takes a lot of time to raise children, and any woman who does is phenomenal. They often feel as though there aren't enough hours in the day to do everything and fit in exercise. Was I ready to commit to that? As I looked around me, I remembered the discussions about how much weight the moms had gained, how hard it was to get off, and the lack of time they had now to dedicate to weight loss. Those pieces all played a part in my decision-making process. It may seem completely selfish (and maybe it is), but when you've put in the time to lose weight and finally feel good about yourself, gaining back the weight during pregnancy factored into my decision not to have children.

Don't get me wrong—there were other factors, too. I wasn't sure I even wanted children or that having children would be best for my husband and me. It took me months to come to a conclusion. I wasn't a woman who had waited her whole life to have children. My husband and I had long talks about what was best for us; we even discussed the idea of adoption and fostering children. In the end, we decided that maybe child-rearing wasn't for us. This is no judgment on people who lose weight and then have children. I've met many people who wouldn't change having their kids for the world. It just wasn't for me. I didn't want to have to lose the weight twice.

After that major decision, my husband asked me if I'd ever considered having surgery to remove the loose skin that was caused by the weight loss. Since reaching my goal was weight was a long and slow journey, much to my chagrin, the skin rebounded better than I'd expected. I was fortunate that even though I had loose, hanging skin from losing a hundred pounds, I could hide it with clothing. I hadn't really thought about surgery, but I decided to look into it and got a plastic surgeon recommendation from friends. The same name kept appearing: Dr. Pousti.

I made an appointment for a consultation. The appointment was in December, and I really wasn't certain about having the surgery. I didn't know what to expect since I'd never met with a plastic surgeon before. In fact, my preconceived notions of what would happen were completely different than the experience I actually had. I'd expected to meet a staff of plastic Barbies who were obsessed with their looks—after all, that's what I saw on reality television. Instead, I met some fantastic people who cared about me and my concerns.

On the day of my consultation, my stomach felt like giant butterflies were swimming in it. My hands were tucked into my pockets as far as I could get them. On top of all that, I found getting undressed in front of a new doctor super uncomfortable.

Dr. Pousti was the best doctor I could have met, and we all know the type of luck I'd had with medical doctors! He was so nice and had a calm spirit, which I needed. His calm demeanor and soft voice quickly soothed my nerves. He asked thoughtful questions and waited while I recited the answers he needed to determine if the procedure was right for me. Dr. Pousti spent a great deal of time talking to me, listening to my worries and my biggest complaints about my body. One of the main questions I had was if I should focus on exercising more. I mean, in my crazy head, I truly thought if I just went to the gym more than three days a week and ran more than five days a week, the skin would disappear. I don't know where I thought the skin would go; I just thought it would go away.

He looked straight at me and said, "You can run a marathon every day of the week, and it won't matter.

You lost all the weight you can possibly lose, no matter how much you go to the gym."

That was an eye-opening moment for me. I'd read plenty of fitness magazines, and the women on the covers were beautiful. *Shouldn't that be what happens to me?* If they could look that fantastic, then I just needed to haunt the gym more. At least, that was my theory. It had never really crossed my mind that I'd done all I could do. Dr. Pousti quietly answered all my questions and then gave me some literature to read. He reassured me that it was normal to feel nervous, but that I'd already done all the hard work.

One of the coolest things Dr. Pousti's office does is allow prospective clients to privately interview others who have had surgery done with him and his team. That simple act meant a lot to me. I got to ask as many questions as I wanted, and none of the answers were prompted. Many of his patients had undergone surgery to remove loose skin. There were also women who had wanted their body parts back where they belonged. No more boobs hanging to the knees. No more loose skin reaching the floor. Each person I met was beautiful—on the inside and out! It was evident that Dr. Pousti's patients loved him and greatly respected him.

What happened next left me laughing for days. There were two other prospective clients in the room with me, as well as the woman answering our questions. There was a big discussion about whether to have saline or silicone implants. The woman answering our questions asked, "Do you want to feel my breasts?" And she lifted up her shirt. The other two women were saying, "Sure, that would be great." Then, there was me: "Nope."

It was so awkward and uncomfortable for me because I'm pretty shy about showing off my own body, let alone poking a stranger's body. I was amazed and in awe that someone could be so comfortable with her body that she didn't give a second thought to lifting her shirt in front of strangers.

That is, until I had my own surgery done. After you have your body fixed to look so amazing, when you've viewed it as being so ugly for so long, you want to show the whole world the results. You are so proud of how much you've accomplished, and now you're no longer hauling around all the excess skin. I get it now. But at that moment during my first consultation, my face had to show great signs of sheer terror and embarrassment.

After I left the office, I climbed into the car with my husband. He asked me what was wrong. I told him the story, and he burst out laughing. He said, "I can only imagine the horrified look on your face while you tried to play it off, cool as a cucumber." (Which I suck at, by the way!)

Later, as I told the story to my friends and family, I couldn't help but laugh. They all thought it was funny as could be. It actually is pretty funny, and you know what, kudos to the women who are willing to show incoming patients all the awesome work Dr. Pousti has done.

It took me quite a few months to decide to move forward with the surgery. I struggled with the idea of removing the skin. I wasn't sure I was a plastic-surgery type of girl. I was worried that I'd become the type of woman who's so uncomfortable with how she looks that she keeps getting plastic surgery over and over again.

In some ways I even felt like I was cheating. After all, if I had the hanging skin removed, did that mean people would think I'd taken a shortcut when it was time to tell my story? It was almost as though I was punishing myself for gaining such a large amount of weight in the first place. I sort of felt the leftover skin was my cross to bear. I wasn't sure it was okay to be rid of that loose skin. I worked through the guilt and self-punishment. It was time to let the fat chick go, and that was a scary, unnerving thought. She had been with me for a long time. Maybe it really *was* time to stretch my wings and fly. When I think of my transformation, I always picture a fat little caterpillar that has become a butterfly. I was no longer that fat caterpillar. I had to use the wings I'd been given and stretch them to fly. Boy oh boy! That was a new and scary place to be.

After I had the skin removed, it took me a long time to recognize myself in the mirror. Body image is such a strange thing. I could finally recognize myself as thinner, but now I was a whole new girl with new shapes. I expected my friends and family to react negatively, but they were incredibly supportive. The demons I had to work through all came from within.

Am I grateful that I had the skin removed? Absolutely. It was the final step to being rid of the fat chick. Whether someone decides to have skin surgery or not is completely cool in my book. I have no judgment either way. It's a personal choice, and I advise anyone considering it to find the right doctor who will help you for the right reasons. Not all plastic surgeons are created equal. There are quite a few of them who want to make a quick buck and will do their best to sell a particular procedure to you. Don't rush and commit to the first doctor you find. Do your research. I was lucky; the doctor I found was completely honest and would only perform the surgery if he felt we were a right fit.

Dr. Pousti is truly a magician. When you're ready to look at surgery options, find your own Dr. Pousti They're out there!

## WARRIOR TIP

It's okay to want to make your body look better. You deserve it! *You are amazing!*

# Adventure #12:

## Advice from a Stranger (a.k.a. Me)

O ne piece of advice can be a hard lesson to learn. Your relationships will change. Every relationship you have works based on certain dynamics. Everyone in your circle of friends has a role they play in those friendships. Whether we want to face it or not, in some relationships, we are the fat chicks. When you go out with your girlfriends, you may be the one who doesn't get hit on. Maybe you're someone's wingwoman.

When you start to become thinner, you suddenly have a different role to play. It doesn't change who you're friends with, but oftentimes it changes the dynamics of the friendship. It may happen in familial relationships, too.

When you've been a certain person for a really long time, and you change the person you are, it can alter the way people see you. Maybe your newfound confidence comes out. Maybe you're a little more outspoken. Maybe you now like taking bigger risks. You *cannot* lose weight and remain the same person. It's like asking a caterpillar to not become a butterfly after it's already wrapped up in its chrysalis. No matter what happens, the caterpillar has to change. It's perfectly okay, too. Like a caterpillar, you will experience some serious transformations—both in yourself and in your relationships.

In fact, in my own marriage, at different points during my journey, my husband looked at me and said, "I don't even know who you are." He was right. I wasn't the same brownie-dough-eating, midnight-nacho-getting, exercise-avoiding chick. Now my life revolved around becoming healthier, eating better, and exercising. It took some time not only for me to get used to the new me, but for everyone around me to get used to it, too. I would often look into the mirror and think, *I don't recognize that girl*. It takes time, patience, and acceptance. You can't stop the freight train of change. But you get to be the conductor of that freight train, so grab your new, smaller conductor's hat and yell, "All aboard!" Those who love and cherish you will jump right up.

I wish I'd known that my body would lose weight in places I didn't think could shed any weight. How could I know that my breasts would get smaller but my butt wouldn't change? Or that I'd have to lose a lot of weight before my legs got smaller? Wherever we lose weight, it's never where we wanted the weight to come off. So hang in there. You will get smaller, and you will be a different shape. After all, round is a shape. Now you can be a smaller round shape!

When someone compliments you about the weight you're losing, just say thank you. We never want to teach others that it isn't okay to give us a compliment. I had such a hard time with this. As I got thinner, people would approach me, saying how great I looked. Almost every time, I'd reply, "Oh, I have much more to lose." It totally negated the nice compliment I'd been paid. By responding in that manner, I gave others the message that it wasn't okay to give me a compliment—and without meaning to, I was also making the giver of the compliment feel awkward.

Now, I'm not saying you have to be all egotistical and act as though you're God's gift to the world (but you could if you wanted to). But accept those nice compliments. You've worked hard and have earned them. Embrace the glory!

What do you do after you reach your dream goal? Do you set another goal? After I reached my weight-loss goal, I moved on to the maintenance phase of my journey. What I learned about the maintenance phase is it's a whole lot harder to maintain the weight loss than it was to lose it in the first place. While in the process of losing it, you have a goal to reach every week. You can gauge some of your success based on what the scale does. You know that if you want to lose more, you have to do more exercise, food monitoring, or both. You have a formula you use to get the weight off. But there's no magic formula to keep it off. I wish I had a magic wand, but I don't.

What I really wish is that at the start of my weight-loss journey, someone had given me advice about what would happen after I hit my goal. Now I'll share the advice I wish others had told me.

Losing weight isn't just about the number. As I reflected on what I'd learned during the process, I felt some major awakenings inside of me. Previously, when I would eat, I did so mindlessly. Eating was where I found my solace and comfort.

At a Weight Watchers classes, I learned about trigger foods and trigger emotions. This means when you see something, you want to eat it, or if you feel a certain way, you want to eat the emotion away. I didn't know what my emotional triggers were.

I really hadn't taken the time to think about emotional eating before that point. What I know about myself now is: "Hello, my name is Suzanne, and I'm an emotional eater." On the days I'm the most tired or out of sorts, I crave chocolate and sugar. Through my pattern tracking, I noticed that right before bedtime, I would stare into the fridge, looking for something to eat. After about my third night in a row doing this—and noticing that it was happening—I finally figured that maybe it was just time to go to bed. Sure enough, as soon as I got into bed, I'd be fast asleep. *Hmm. . . . Maybe there's something to this.*

A few weeks later, I noticed the same eating pattern show up. What an exciting thing to learn about yourself. It's exciting not because it focuses on your flaws, but because it gives you a chance to make a different choice. Now, when I stand in front of the fridge, I logically think, *Am I really hungry, or am I bored or tired?* Realizing that about myself has carried me through difficult times. Whenever my life is full of stress or change, I can't hide myself in the bottom of a bag of chocolate chips. As much as I'd love to sit on my couch and eat all the chocolate I want, I am no longer that person. The knowledge I now have empowers me to make different choices. Knowledge truly is power.

There are two answers to every question I ask. Number one, I pray to get an answer. Prayer is where I started my journey, and from it is where I continue get my strength. If prayer isn't for you, use whatever it is that helps you be strong. Is it nature? Is it interactions with friends or family? One thing I learned through my prayer and experiences is that I can't hang on to all the sadness, grief, anger, loneliness, or whatever emotion I experience that makes me turn to food. If I hang on to those emotions, I'll continue to fall back into the same deadly traps as before. I can't be stuck in those traps. Instead, as a way to combat those traps, I found my second answer, which is to serve others.

I've learned that I can't be sick and tired of being sick and tired, *and* serve others at the same time. To serve others, you must take the focus off yourself and instead focus on helping others. Doing this helped me to take my focus off of food. Think about it like this: If you extend your hand to others, there is no place to focus other than on the other person. If you hold your hand in a closed fist, you can't help but look internally. The mere act of extending a hand will shift energy from you to someone else.

When I'm struggling with an emotion and want to turn to food, I extend my hand to help others. Now, that doesn't mean it isn't still about food. Maybe I'll take what's tempting me and give it to the local food pantry. Maybe I'll use it to bake for others, which is my favorite option. The mere act of giving and knowing that the baked goods I make will help others makes me want to stop focusing on myself and my weight. And as a side bonus, I've learned that if I can get the dough or batter into the oven and baked, I don't want to eat it. No raw cookie dough or refrigerated brownie mix hiding out in the fridge for me any longer!

I can't stress enough the importance of serving others. The next time you are struggling with an emotion that makes you want to eat, research a charity with which you'd like to work. Maybe find a food pantry where you can serve food to those in need. Or go to an animal shelter and offer to walk dogs. The act of service will get you out of the house and helping others. It's a win-win situation.

I found it out completely by accident. Around Christmas to New Year's is a hard time for me when it comes to avoiding snacks and chocolate. Isn't that when all the Oreos start floating around? Since I love to bake, I decided to create trays of cookies for the less fortunate. Don't get me wrong—I know cookies aren't the best food choice, but around the holidays, some people don't get any treats or presents. I decided that instead of eating it all, I'd do something good with it.

Baking surely isn't the answer for everyone. But it's my way to give back. Find what works for you. I think giving back to the community is a super important piece of the journey. It helped me with my weight-loss journey, and I hope it helps you and those around you, too.

Invisibility is something I thought only happened to me. But I met many people on their own weight-loss journeys who have had similar experiences or stories. I'm sure it's more obvious to women because we typically *want* to be noticed in public. It's important that we look good and that someone thinks we're attractive; it's something that's almost been bred into us.

But one day, a dear friend of mine explained the phenomenon to me. I told him my perspective of being invisible, and he shared his perspective of heavier women. He explained that your size doesn't matter when you enter a public place. To men, what matters is how women carry themselves as they enter. If you notice someone who is thinner and carries herself confidently, then men will likely notice her. He reiterated that it isn't the size that attracts men to a woman. *It's what she exudes from her inner being.*

It took me some time to digest that. I thought back to when I was heavy and would sometimes feel as though I were invisible. Did I carry myself like I was all that and a bag of potato chips, or did I try to blend in with the wallpaper? I'm pretty certain I had imaginary wallpaper flowers all over me in just about every instance.

As we lose weight, our confidence grows. We become surer of ourselves, and it shows in all we do. The way you behave or carry yourself is how others will perceive you. Our confidence or lack thereof shows up during job interviews, dates, and within relationships. I often wonder how many women feel they're "not enough" because of their weight. Ironically, it isn't your weight that defines you. It is *who you are* that defines you. Now, I'm not saying you should be super happy while at your heaviest because I suck at lying. I know that when you're heavy and you want to be thinner, pretending to be happy is crap. We always want to be somewhere else. But what I am saying is, instead of being ashamed or embarrassed about your current weight, *own* the weight you're at and focus on what you *can* do, who you are, your amazing abilities, and what goals you want to achieve. These focal points will help you better appreciate yourself. As my friend so eloquently put it, "Size doesn't matter. Self-confidence and self-esteem are what matter."

How do you carry yourself? Are you a victor or a victim? Be a victor so you can have the life you've always dreamed of.

One of the things I had the hardest time accepting was that I was skinnier and looked different. The name of this phenomenon is "phantom fat." This is when you still see yourself as the larger, heavier version of yourself even though you have a smaller, thinner body. Not only were there times I didn't recognize myself, there were also times I still saw myself as the fat chick. Even though I was skinnier than I'd been in years, I had trouble recognizing it. I still felt I looked like the 256-pound person trying to wedge herself into too-small clothes.

When my friends would tell me how good I looked, I'd always say thanks and then something like, "I still have a long way to go." I just couldn't see it. In fact, if there were two people standing close together, talking, and I needed to squeeze behind them to sit down, I'd walk the long way around them because I still viewed myself as the fat chick who couldn't fit between those two people.

It took me a long time to become spatially aware with my new body. One of my friends used the analogy of driving a U-Haul truck and then getting behind the wheel of a VW bug. It would take time to get used to how much smaller the bug is than the U-Haul. It's the same way with your brain; it takes a little while to recognize the smaller version of you. Be patient with your brain. When you realize you can fit in smaller spaces, be proud! It took a lot of time and effort to get there.

Along those same lines, I remember the first time I didn't have to shop in the plus-sized department of a clothing store. When I would enter a store, I'd automatically walk to the section for heavier women. But I reached the point that I had to shop where the smaller sizes were kept. At first, it was so foreign to me; it felt weird. I had to become okay with the fact that just because I bought smaller clothing sizes, it didn't mean I'd suddenly go to back to weighing 256 pounds, as if those smaller clothes had magic powers that made a person fat! In fact, the day

I finally got to shop at Victoria's Secret, I almost bought out the store. Lingerie stores didn't carry clothes in my previous size, so it was a new experience to shop in those types of stores. So long, big-box stores! Momma's getting some new, smaller panties!

Know that it's normal to have to learn your new size. You'll eventually come to accept yourself as a thinner version of you, but it will take time. Don't sabotage yourself in the process.

At some point after I lost a hundred pounds, I was talking with my aunt about my weight loss. She was discouraged about her weight and said, "I wish I had what you have." Those words took a little while to sink in. I spent some time pondering about "what I had." The truth of the matter is that I don't have any special superpower or magical gift that no one else has. The difference is that I'm tapping into my own power to become stronger and live longer.

Each of us has the power to persevere. Each of us can choose to make a difference in our lives as well as the lives of those around us. You don't have to sit around wishing you had strength. You don't have to wish you could be someone or something. You already have that ability. Too often, we give our power away to others—to temptation, to just sitting on our butts doing nothing. *You have the power.* I think about the play *Wicked*, where Glinda says, "You already have the power in you." That is so incredibly true. You already have all the power, fortitude, and strength you need to reach your weight goals.

Power is inside us. It drives us to do whatever we want. Power is what drives you to get up in the morning. We get to choose where and how to use our power. I don't believe I'm the only one with the power to lose weight. We all have it. Sometimes it's buried deep, and sometimes it's shrouded in self-doubt; but the power is there. My hope is that each of us sees the power we have inside ourselves and chooses to use it.

We often recognize power in others, but we doubt our own. Those who you watch and hope to imitate are just like you. They simply tapped into their power a little sooner. Don't wait to tap into yours! Make the choice to use your power now. Choose to make your life and the world around you better by tapping into your personal power and becoming healthier, thinner, and more confident. You already have it in you. She-Ra is already inside of you!

At first, I didn't recognize how much of an accomplishment it was to lose a hundred pounds. When I'd tell people about my weight loss, their next question was always, "How did you do it?" After that, they'd ask, "How long have you kept it off?" At first, I didn't understand the seriousness of those questions. I assumed everyone could lose that kind of weight.

I was talking with one of my friends, and he said, "Do you know what a big deal that is?" I stared at him and said, "No." I really didn't. It seemed like a normal thing; I just assumed anyone could do it. My friend talked about how most people give up when they reach a setback. I hadn't really thought about that. I'd just known that going back to that weight wasn't an option for me.

So, what keeps me from gaining it back? The mere thought of having to purchase bigger clothes. Being okay with being heavy is not an option in my life. That doesn't mean that I don't fall off the wagon. It *does* mean there is now a weight where I draw a line in the sand—and it's long before I reach 256 pounds. I think everyone has a line they draw and say, "Enough is enough."

Don't think I only eat salads and plain chicken because that's not the case. I am a normal person who likes to eat out and indulge on snacks at Disneyland. But I'm no longer the person who can sit and eat an entire box of brownie mix. I must choose to recognize my triggers and make a logical decision to stop. You can do the same thing.

What's your breaking point? What's your catalyst, making you say, "Enough is enough"? I hear all the time about people who quit smoking cold turkey, so we all know it's possible. The question is: Do you *believe* it's possible for you? Do you want to be thinner as badly as you want to breathe? It's the moment you answer affirmatively that you can tap into your power.

I didn't know I was shirking my power when people asked about my weight-loss story. In fact, sometimes I was hesitant to talk about it because I didn't want to be perceived as the "food police." I pass no judgment on what you eat. I can't travel your journey, just like others couldn't travel mine.

But what I can do is share my story so people can realize they have a rockstar inside of them—and she's waiting to be released. How long will you wait to release her? I finally faced mine and began sharing my story. Was it easy? Hell, no. Was it frustrating and difficult? Hell, yeah! Does any amount of food taste as good as how fitting into my skinny jeans feels? No way.

I have a line in the sand. Have you drawn yours?

Sometimes the experiences you go through on a journey are difficult, but when you look back, it seems almost unbelievable. I was on a conference phone call one day when someone asked, "If you could do anything in the world, what would it be?" I didn't really have an answer. I was at a point where I felt lost. I didn't know who I was. I was having trouble identifying what I wanted to do. I'd been the fat chick for so long that I didn't know what to do with the skinny girl. I truly felt like a lost soul.

Most people I knew had answers for the question I'd been asked. Maybe they wanted to be rock stars, or millionaires or whatever, but I didn't have a clue. I hung up the phone and cried. As I sat in my chair at my desk, a thought occurred to me. *What if I were a motivational speaker? How many lives could I impact?* I just shook my head and thought, *Right. Who am I, the next Joyce Meyers? Not a chance.*

It was intriguing to me, though. The thought of helping other people see that they could lose weight, too. The very thought of speaking and helping others made my heart race. Where had this big idea come from? Was it God whispering in my ear?

About two weeks later, someone called me about attending a seminar on accepting yourself and achieving your calling. I hadn't heard of the seminar before, but I knew I needed some guidance on how to help others. I was lost and lonely. I couldn't think straight, and I didn't know what to do with my weight loss. In the middle of the training, we were directed to come up, stand on a chair, and say our names. How hard could that be?

I couldn't do it. I got to the chair and just stood there. I went to climb up and burst into tears. Here it was: I was supposed to stand up and say my name, and I couldn't even do it. I wanted to be a public speaker and tell others my story, but I couldn't even utter my name. It was a horrible experience and a transforming one at the same time.

Through those exercises, I learned that even though I felt I was broken, I could still make a difference in people's lives. I'm very blessed to be able to share my story with you. I feel super lucky that I had that experience—where I stood, vulnerable, in front of a crowd, and slowly started to speak my name.

About two weeks later, I joined Toastmasters. I needed to find a way to tell my story without breaking down in tears. I wanted to be able to help others in their weight-loss journeys. It all started with me. After that first meeting, I told my husband that I wanted to become a speaker. Talk about the deer-in-the-headlights look. I'm sure I caused utter panic and confusion in his world. But he understood that my need to help others is huge.

One of the first speaking assignments I did was to share my story with a few Weight Watchers groups. It was terribly scary at first. One of the largest obstacles I had to overcome was showing my "before weight loss" picture. In one of the first speeches, I showed it to the audience for, like, half a second. My Weight Watchers leader asked, "Do you mind showing that again?" So I did. In my mind, it wasn't about my before picture. It was about telling the audience to stick with their weight-loss journey. Little did I know that people wanted the picture to *believe* that they could lose the weight, too. Isn't that what we're all looking for? Someone like us who has lost the weight and can identify with how we feel and what is happening? I'm not ashamed of how much I weighed or what I looked like before. It's part of my story—just like where you are right now is part of your story.

I was so nervous the first few speeches that I stammered and stuttered. At one point, I asked for questions from the audience. I thought the people would have some deep, profound questions. Instead what I received was, "Am I ever going to be able to eat real food? Or am I destined to eating only lettuce my whole life?" That question still makes me laugh. Why? Because I understand exactly where that person was coming from because I've been there, wondering if I was going to have to eat only lettuce to drop the weight. I know that deep down, what they were asking was, "How long am I going to have to do this diet thing?" Everyone always wants to know how I lost the weight. How long did it take me? I know people want a quick fix, but I don't have the answer for that. If I knew a quick fix, it wouldn't have taken me four years!

At another speaking engagement, I talked to a group about how the road to weight loss isn't easy. But if you keep at it, it will pay off. As I spoke, I saw a woman, in the back of the audience, who was dabbing at her eyes. After I concluded my speech, the woman approached me and said she'd stepped on the scale that morning and she was frustrated. She told me that hearing my talk had helped her see that it's okay if it takes a little while to lose the weight.

In that moment, I discovered *I have the ability to make a difference*. I am here to tell you that it is *possible*. You don't need to wonder if you can lose the weight. You don't have to worry that it's impossible because it isn't. You are meant to make a difference in this world. You are the rock star in this story.

What if someone is waiting on you to make a decision before they take a chance on you? What if someone is waiting for you to be the pebble in the pond that creates an ever-widening circle, impacting others? What if who you're meant to be is waiting for you to take that first step? Why would you allow the weight to hold you back from being the grandest, most amazing, balls-out person ever imagined? It doesn't have to. You can make the choice to change it. Right here. Right now.

What are you waiting for?

# Adventure #13:

## The End of the Journey... Or, Is It?

---

I t took me a while to realize the impact my weight loss had on others. I came home to see my family one time, and my stepdad had lost quite a bit of weight. I was and am so proud of him because he'd been having blood sugar issues, and I know it isn't easy to lose weight. When I walked through the door, I gave him a giant hug and told him how great he looked! He hugged me back and said, "You inspired me."

Even thinking about that interaction now makes me feel like crying tears of happiness. I wasn't trying to make a statement to my family or anyone. I was just trying to take care of myself. It was one of those moments that my own actions quietly made an impact on other's lives. I don't have to stand on a mountaintop and tell everyone how to live their lives. Instead, I can just be me, and you can just be you, too.

So many times in life, our friends and families watch us, living vicariously through us. Sometimes, they might even wish they were us. They look up to us for our courage and tenacity. It's in the quiet moments that people think maybe they can do what you're doing.

You are giving someone around you hope that they can reach their goals. You are standing strong for yourself and others. Don't for a moment take for granted that you inspire others. To you, going for a thirty-minute walk may seem like a minor thing. But to someone around you, it might be scary to walk for five minutes. Because of your example, someone will gain the strength and determination to try something new. You are somebody's rock star. Because of you, someone can get up today and make it a better day. Embrace that!

When times get tough and you want to give up, remember that you need to keep going because you make a difference. You may never know who you'll impact, but dig deep anyway. Then dig a little deeper! Be the person to whom someone can say, "Because of you, I didn't quit!" Be bold. Show the world your greatness!

It was during that moment with my stepdad that I learned my true calling: to be the voice of hope for a broken, overweight world.

Quite a few people have told me that I should write a book about my experience. But it was never on my to-do list. In fact, I put it off for a long time. I didn't think people would really want to hear my story.

One day, I was sitting and people-watching, and I heard a couple of women talking about weight loss. It was as though I was hearing my old self speaking. Even though I wasn't the fat chick anymore, I'd been in the exact spot they talked about, which dealt with frustration, self-sabotage, and giving up. I began to wonder if my story could help others.

Most who are on a weight-loss journey don't think it's possible to lose a lot of weight. The stories I usually read were about women who only had a small amount of weight to lose, or they lost their weight in a short amount of time. I didn't know anyone else who'd lost the amount of weight I did. After all, it wasn't as though morbid obesity ran in my family. Then it hit me. *I can be the example for those people who are looking for inspiration. I can be the pebble in the pond of life.* Wow! That was truly eye-opening and created a way I could serve others.

My goal for writing this book was not so I could be proud and talk all about me. My goal was to share the hard lessons I'd learned. Hopefully by reading about my experiences, others wouldn't have to learn the hard way, like I had. I have screwed up diets and exercises about as much as a person can. I have eaten it all and lived to tell about it. *Life is all about the journey*. We can rush to the finish line of whatever goal we're shooting for, *or* we can start walking toward our goal, taking pictures and collecting stories along the way.

In my heart, I believe it's through the experiences we have that we learn the most about ourselves. We spend much time being moms, sisters, aunts, cousins, and wives. Too often we get so caught up in being those roles that when life settles down, we sit back and say to ourselves, "Who am I?" As we travel the journey of life, the experiences we have make us who we are.

Don't rush toward the finish line. Stop. Walk. Take pictures. Because part of the journey is about the person we become along the way. Sure, we could go on some super-high-profile, half-a-grapefruit-a-day diet and lose twenty pounds in three days. Or we could take the longer, sometimes harder approach to greatness and learn who we are in the process. I chose route number two, and I'm glad I did. If I had run to the finish, I wouldn't be able to become inspired by those who read my book and who I've met along the way. After all, the point of the journey isn't that we finished. The point is that we had the courage to even start.

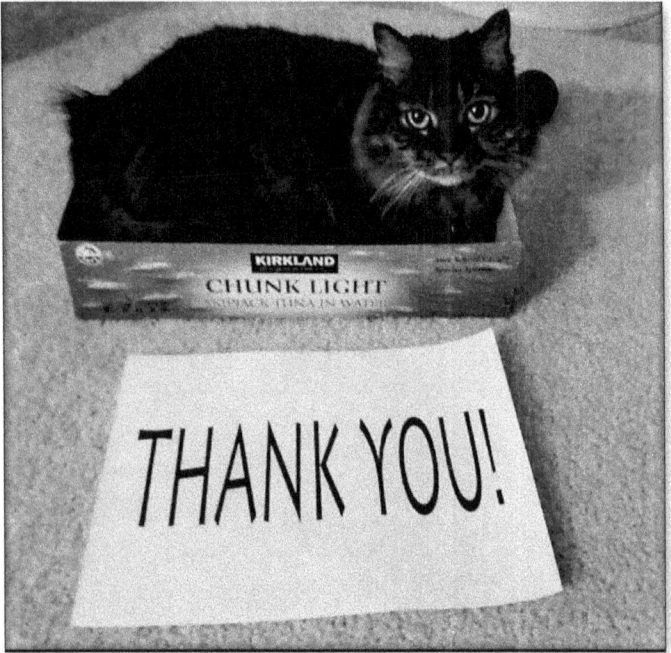

(shameless use of my cat, Spanky!)

# URGENT REQUEST!

---

**Thank You For Reading My Book!**

I love hearing what you have to say, (both the good and the bad!), and your input is very important to me.

Please take a few minutes and leave me a helpful review on Amazon letting me know what you thought of the book. This feedback from real people like you hclps me become a better author.

Thanks so much!
—Suzanne Berkey

# Acknowledgements

I certainly didn't get here on my own. To each of you and many others, I am forever grateful for your help, your encouragement, and your belief that this whole thing was possible.

My Husband, Jeff, thanks for all your behind the scenes help, love and support and especially for being my cheerleader. All those times when I was lost, you helped me find my way.

My parents, Linda and Farley Hicks, and Mike and Penney Clark, thanks for your love and support. The laughter along this journey has been great and that's what life is supposed to be about. Thank you!

My BFF, Wendy Allen, thanks for your fun and laughter. Without you, who knows what the title of this book would be? Your insight has been amazing, and you have been a rockstar in this big journey. All those times laughing on the floor of the shoe department paid off!

The girls, Cora Afonien and Tami Depasse, thanks for letting me tell you all my big plans while you smiled so graciously. Tami, thanks for the edit and the supporting words as I wrote this book. It was so desperately needed!

My chaps, Janice Scarlett and Elsa Celio, thanks for the long walks with amazing talks. Because of you, I kept sane (well, I tried), and your great insights help me to see the light! Thank you for all the laughs! You really do give moist hearts!

My aunt, Nancy Edsall, thanks for the support along in this journey as well as the editing that you did. You are an amazing cheerleader, not only to me, but to all the family. You make an impact!

I also want to thank, (I feel like this is an Academy Awards speech)..Matt Kramer and Remi Malahieude, thanks for the kick in the pants that I needed to get this all in book format. Without our meetings each week, who knows where this story would be! You both have been invaluable.

Kim Eisenhaur-Pierce, thanks for being the most amazing weight loss cheerleader a girl could ask for. Dr. Bruce Shin, without you helping me along the way, I would still be stuck in the same spot in my life. Your help has changed my life forever. I am forever grateful to Dr. Tom Pousti. Thank you for all that you did to help me see my beauty. Your gentleness and patience was a BIG DEAL! You showed up at the perfect time with your gentle spirit!

To all the V5 crew, the mentors and the coaches, Daniel and Kim, thanks for helping me find my warrior within me and learning to not be afraid to be a rockstar. Because of you, I am able to say my name and spread my love to the world!  You all are an amazing group of people.  I am lucky to have had such an experience with you!

Lastly, thanks to Palmetto Publishing Group for your help in organizing me, editing me, and just being awesome in answering my unending first time author questions.  Without your encouragement, I would still be an author with a story in my head.

# About Me

I'm a former fat chick and struggled with my weight for most of my life. After an eye-opening incident I'll never forget, I took the first step on my weight-loss journey. I walked thousands of miles, made many lifestyle changes, came to some difficult realizations about myself, and at the end of it all, I had successfully lost 100 pounds. Eight years later, I decided to share my story with you by writing *The Day My Shorts Fit My Dad*.

Losing a significant amount of weight wasn't an easy feat to accomplish. I ran into obstacles along the way, among them, hiding chocolate in the bottom of the freezer so I couldn't see it, and my doctor labeling me morbidly obese. Together with my husband and two cats, I've put in lots of miles and races to continue my journey, and I look forward to many more.

My dream is to hear from you, walk with you, share laughs and tears with you. To know that maybe my story helped you take that one more step to continue your own journey. Because *you are a rock star*!

Email me at
suzanne@thewarriorwithinme.com,
and be sure to check out my blog for
motivational tips, humor, and prizes!

You can find it at
www.thewarriorwithinme.com.

www.ingramcontent.com/pod-product-compliance
Lightning Source LLC
Chambersburg PA
CBHW070808050426
42452CB00011B/1954